Designed by:
Constantine Odongo
UCU Alumnus

Edited and Co-ordinated by:
Patty Huston-Holm and Eleanor Ithungu

CONTENTS

- **2** Message from the Deputy Vice Chancellor of Academic Affairs
- **4** Message from the Vice Chancellor
- **5** UCU Vision, Mission, Core Values
- **6** Why choose Uganda Christian University
- **7** Locations of Uganda Christian University constituent colleges
- **10** Student Affairs and Services
- **12** University Governance
- **13** Financial Aid and Scholarships
- **14** The Chaplaincy
- **15** Other Programmes and Services

PROGRAMMES

- **21** Bishop Tucker School of Theology
- **27** Faculty of Business and Administration
- **41** Faculty of Education and Arts
- **51** Faculty of Journalism, Communication and Media Studies
- **55** Faculty of Law
- **71** Faculty of Science and Technology
- **83** Faculty of Social Sciences
- **93** School of Medicine

- **102** School of Research and Postgraduate Studies
- **103** Instruments of Identity

JOHN MULINDWA KITAYIMBWA

MESSAGE FROM THE DEPUTY VICE CHANCELLOR OF ACADEMIC AFFAIRS

Greetings from Uganda Christian University (UCU), the Centre of Excellence in the Heart of Africa! We are passionate about offering our students a stimulating and rich curriculum, which integrates faith in learning, gives them required skills and inspires them to provide solutions in the world God places them. Sports, music and leadership opportunities round out the campus experience to best prepare our graduates for various careers and for serving others around the world. Needless to say, our students have the opportunity to make use of their potential to develop academic, creative, social and Christian livelihoods.

We offer more than 100 programmes with approximately 1,000 courses in eight faculty areas: Business and Administration, Education and Arts, Law, Science and Technology, Medicine, Social Sciences, Theology and Divinity, and Journalism, Communication and Media Studies. Education at UCU is filled with academic, professional and research experiences to excite and motivate learners to succeed.

Explore this catalogue of programmes and consider Uganda Christian University for your educational advancement.

[www.ucu.ac.ug]

THE DEPUTY VICE CHANCELLOR, DEVELOPMENT, EXTERNAL RELATIONS AND FINANCE

DAVID MUGAWE

THE REV. CANON DR. JOHN SENYONYI

MESSAGE FROM THE VICE CHANCELLOR

Everywhere I go, I bump into Uganda Christian University (UCU) graduates - lawyers, accountants, pastors, teachers, social workers and more. Besides, employers too testify that UCU's graduates bring a unique, desirable addition to their workforce. That employers hire UCU alumni more readily than graduates from other universities is one testament to the quality education we have provided since 1997.

An even more important testament is the intentional Christ-centredness at UCU. Christian faith and values are embedded in all we say and do. Not only do we offer traditional university sports and other extra-curricular activities, but worship and Bible studies are frequent throughout the five campuses as are course-integrated biblical teachings. Most programmes reinforce community engagement alongside classroom theoretical learning. We expect students to use virtue, knowledge and skill to serve others, as our Lord and Saviour would want. This has been the branding of UCU since its inception more than two decades ago.

Study at UCU is a community experience, helping every student to belong and feel welcome into the UCU Family. UCU's education is truly "universal," as a university's education should be. Hence our catchphrase, which aptly summarises UCU's brand, namely, "A Complete Education for A Complete Person."

I've seen this first-hand since coming to UCU as the first full-time University Chaplain in 2001. Three years later, in 2004, UCU became the first private university in Uganda's higher education history to be issued a charter. UCU has registered several other firsts. For example, UCU becoming the first university in our country to legally register a constituent college, Bishop Barham University College in 2007, followed by Mbale University College in 2016. And it was the first university in Uganda to host the Inter-University Games twice, at both the national and regional levels.

The university that began exclusively with studies in the Humanities has gradually expanded into the Sciences without losing the excellence UCU is now well known for. The recent UCU School of Medicine is a demonstration of this. All her programmes are competitively sought after.

As UCU continues to grow and adjust her curriculum to remain relevant to today's world and its needs, and as we garner attention to our enviable reputation and the research in issues of importance, we never lose sight of our focus on Christ and his teachings. For Jesus is LORD and so, UCU shall continue to be a university of first choice.

To God be the glory.

[www.ucu.ac.ug]

Values

CHRIST-CENTREDNESS
We acknowledge the Lordship of Christ, seeking to know and obey God's will, challenging ingrained secular thinking in education.

DILIGENCE
We are careful in whatever we do, conscientious at work and persistent in the face of difficulty because our work is a service to Lord Jesus Christ.

INTEGRITY
We hold to sound moral character, as defined by biblical principles of upholding honesty and transparency, truthfulness, faithfulness and exercising humility.

SERVANTHOOD
We are convinced that all people bear the image of God; therefore we commit to love them as we love ourselves, using our positions of influence to build up others.

STEWARDSHIP
We faithfully manage ourselves, our relationship and tangible resources knowing that these are given to us in trust, for God's glory.

UGANDA CHRISTIAN UNIVERSITY
A Centre of Excellence in the Heart of Africa

Vision
○ A Centre of Excellence in the Heart of Africa

Mission
○ A To equip students for productive, holistic lives of the Christian faith and service

[www.ucu.ac.ug]

WHY UGANDA CHRISTIAN UNIVERSITY?

Uganda Christian University is a private, not-for-profit post-secondary institution established by the Church of Uganda, part of the global communion of churches descended from the Anglican Church, in 1997. It grew from Bishop Tucker Theological College that started in 1913.

As founded by the Church of Uganda, UCU's Chancellor is the Archbishop. The Rt. Rev. Dr. Stephen Samuel Kaziimba is the 9th Archbishop and the fourth UCU Chancellor, replacing the Most Rev. Stanley Ntagali in March 2020.

Following the service of the Rt. Rev. Eliphaz Maari as acting vice-chancellor in the first two years of the university, the two vice chancellors have been the Rev. Dr. Stephen Noll (2000-2010) and the Rev. Canon Dr. John Senyonyi (2010-2020).

Among the many highlights in UCU's 22 years are:
• In 2003, the Kampala, Mbale and Arua campuses start.
• In 2004, UCU is chartered as the first private university in Uganda.
• In 2007, Bishop Barham University College is registered as a constituent college of UCU.
• In 2011, the main Ham Musaka Library opens.
• In 2012, the main campus science labs open.
• In 2016, UCU signs an MoU with Mengo Hospital to start a medical school.
• In 2017, construction starts to improve facilities at the Kampala campus.

Since its inception, the university has grown from four to the current eight main curriculum areas – Business, Education/Arts, Law, Science and Technology, Medicine, Social Science, Theology, Journalism/Communications housed in eight main faculties and schools throughout the university. Within this area, there are more than 100 diploma-to-master's degree programmes with highly qualified instructors and a proven track record of graduate employment.

The university also is especially unique because of its emphasis on integrating Christian faith and learning as well as reinforcing a strong character-building atmosphere based on Christian ethics and principles.

Ntagali

Kaziimba

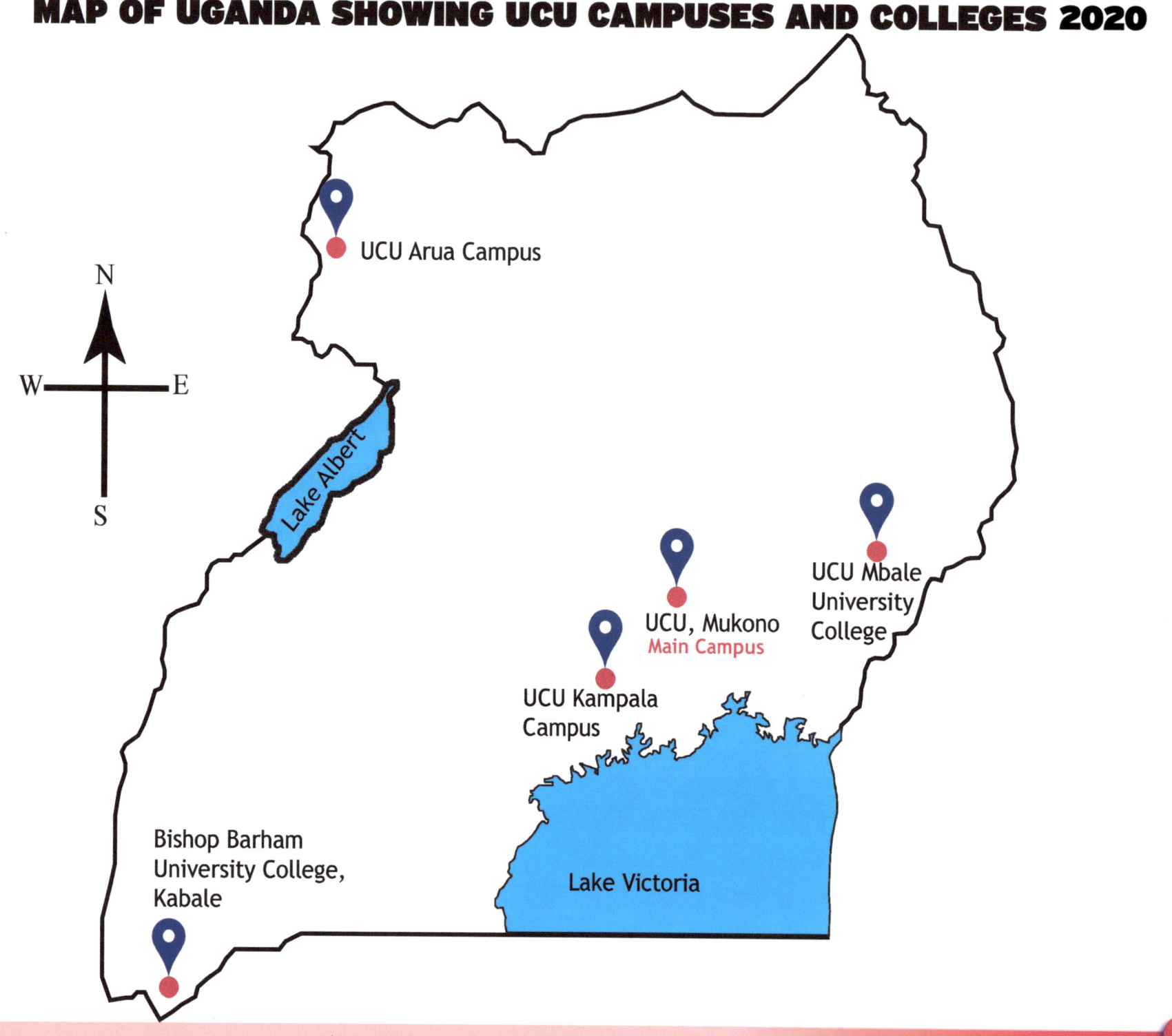

ADMISSION AT UCU

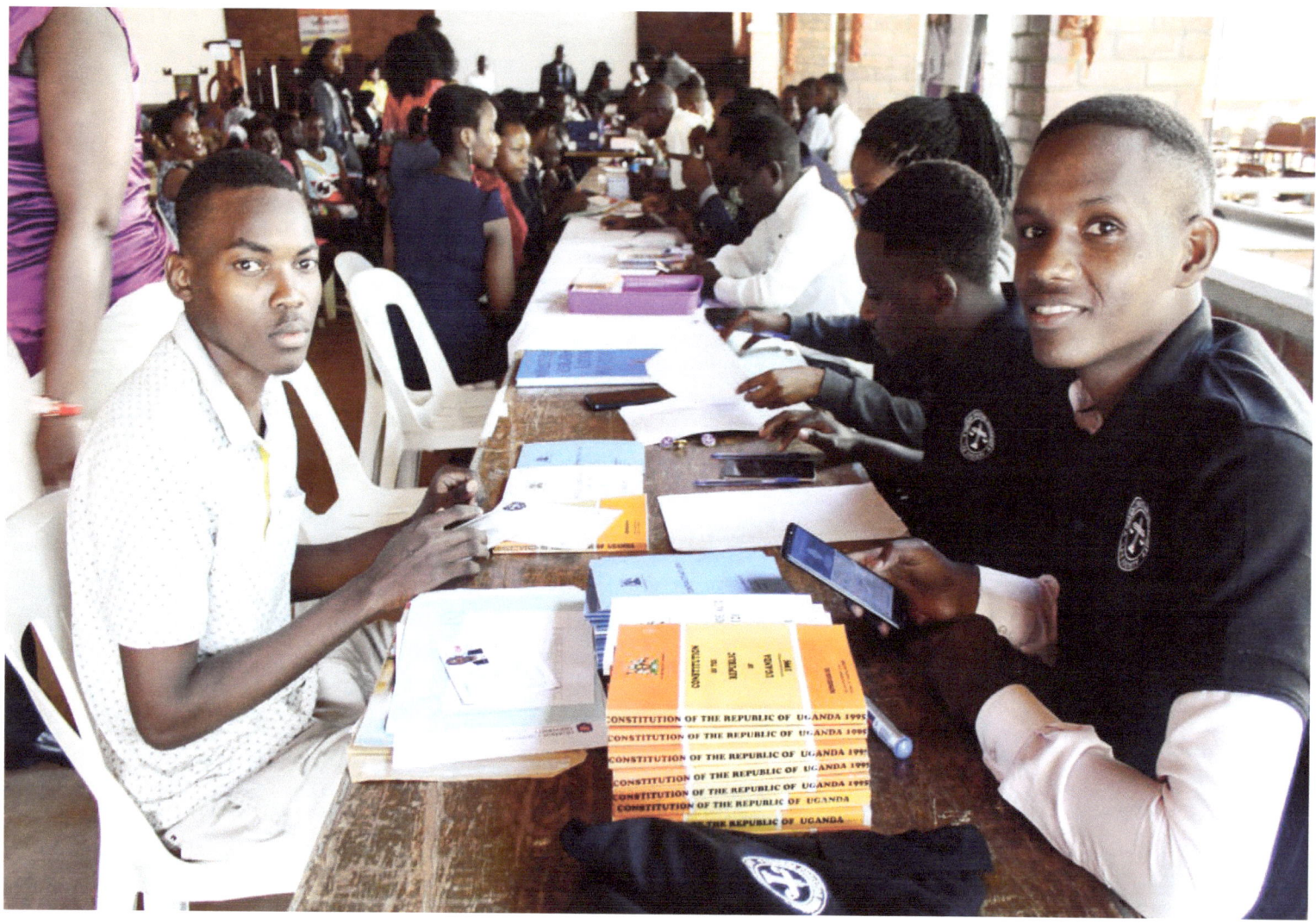

The UCU student application form can be obtained from the university website (click on "How to Apply" at https://ucu.ac.ug/) or obtained at the Main Campus, Bishop Barham University College, Kabale and the campuses of Mbale and Arua.

Application forms may also be obtained from the diocesan education offices of Busoga, Soroti, Ankole, North Ankole, and Bunyoro-Kitara.

The application form must contain all required information and be accompanied by relevant academic documents and a non-refundable application fee of Shs50,000 or $25. It must be returned to the Admissions Office of the university according to the set deadline dates.

Semesters and their starting periods are: Advent (September), Easter (January), and Trinity (May).

THE ADMISSIONS OFFICE
Uganda Christian University,
P. O. Box 4 Mukono, Uganda.
Telephone: +256312350880/835
Mobile: +256794770826
Email: *admissions@ucu.ac.ug*

STUDENTS AFFAIRS AND SERVICES

Culture

While courses are taught in English, there are opportunities to learn about other cultures and to reinforce the value of one's own mother tongue. One activity that is co-ordinated by the Guild in co-operation with the DOSA is a cultural gala with costuming, music and acting

The person in charge of the Directorate of Student Affairs is the Director of Student Affairs (DOSA). Whether at the Mukono main campus or studying from Kampala, Arua, Mbale or Kabale campuses, assistance and services are provided in six main areas.

1. Student Affairs – From topical discussions to engagement in cultural celebrations, students have opportunities to grow intellectually, ethically and socially. The Student Guild leadership works closely with university leaders to share student concerns and to communicate information from faculties.

> **Not forsaking our own assembling together, but encouraging one another..."** Hebrews 10:25

> **Love your neighbour as yourself. There is no commandment greater than this** Mark 12:31.

2. International Students – From countries throughout Africa and occasionally other continents, students come to UCU for curricular and cultural enrichment. This office serves as a bridge to create comfort in a home away from home. One long-standing programme is the Uganda Studies Program whereby hundreds of mostly American students in more than a decade have engaged in one semester each of study under the Council for Christian Colleges and Universities.

3. Sports and Recreation – Organized sports at Uganda Christian University include basketball, volleyball, tennis, badminton, netball, soccer, woodball, tae-kwon-do, rugby, swimming, aerobics, table tennis and handball. Less active activities such as chess and scrabble also are part of the offerings. Scholarships are offered to outstanding athletes. The university has a reputation as having the top teams in East Africa.

> **Do you not know that your bodies are temples of the Holy Spirit, who is in you, whom you have received from God? . . .Therefore, honour God with your bodies** 1 Corinthians 6: 19-20

4. Counselling and Wellness – Individual, family and group counselling are offered for staff and students. Among issues handled are: Fear, anxiety, stress, depression, grief, trauma, anger management, addiction and relationships. Workshops are offered on such topics as parenting, marriage and substance abuse.

> **Cast all your anxieties on Him because He cares for you.** 1 Peter: 5-7.

> **When you lie down, you will not be afraid; when you lie down, your sleep will be sweet.**
> **Proverbs 3:24**

5. Accommodation – Hostels on- and off-campus are managed by Uganda Christian University. Student living quarters, including Honours College lodging for high academically performing students, are monitored for safety and sanitation. Those living on campus have access to the Internet, a library and a health centre.

6. Catering – Students choosing a meal plan have the opportunity to eat five times a day with breakfast, tea break, lunch, evening tea, and dinner. Meals include fresh vegetables, rice and meats. Safe, portable drinking water is available. There are several canteens that also provide meals and snacks.

> **Day by day continuing with one mind in the temple, and breaking bread from house to house, they were taking meals together with gladness and sincerity of heart.**
> **Acts 2:46**

UNIVERSITY GOVERNANCE

Uganda President Yoweri Museveni visiting UCU at a past graduation

Uganda Christian University (UCU) is governed by Registered Trustees of the Province of the Church of Uganda through the Provincial Assembly. The university operates in accordance with the laws of the Republic of Uganda. It fulfilled the Ministry of Education and Sports requirements of setting up a university and received a provision licence in 1997. UCU satisfied the National Council for Higher Education requirements of being a credited university and, in 2004, received a charter from the President of Uganda.

While the Church of Uganda Archbishop serves as Chancellor and the Vice Chancellor is the official academic, administrative and financial officer of UCU, the chief governing body is the University Council, which establishes policy and appoints full-time staff. Three main boards that report to the Council involve finance, staff welfare, and planning and development.

The University Senate establishes and awards degrees, adopts academic policy and regulates admissions and examinations.

SCHOLARSHIPS AT UCU

Save a Buddy: Students work to get partial fees for their peers.

Sports: This is mainly awarded to exceptionally good sports students who are members of teams.

Theological: The university gets two students from each diocese across the country under this scholarship.

Work-based: Needy students work throughout the semester to get money accredited to their account commensurate to the amount of work done.

Merit-based: This award is based on academic performance of students. It targets best performing students who are unable to pay tuition at the university.

Biological: These benefit children of full-time staff at UCU.

Mark Bartels, executive director, UCU Partners

FINANCIAL AID & SCHOLARSHIPS

The fundamental objective of the Uganda Christian University (UCU) financial aid office is to co-ordinate different scholarship programmes that benefit students. Private and non-profit entities assist with fundraising for scholarships. The university maintains a list of organisations and individual contributors known as Friends of UCU. Key among these is UCU Partners, a USA-based non-profit-making body founded in 2000.

With the growing need for financial support in the university, the Financial Aid Office in 2019 undertook steps to launch a student loan scheme to ease the hardship and help more students attain their education.

I will go back to my hospital and deliver holistic nursing care to the people within and outside the hospital, with interest in maternal and child health for the betterment of our community and nation... **Uwimbabazi Sarah, nursing, scholarship recipient**

I want to help other needy people in our society by offering and giving back to them what God has done for me... **Ochora Walter, logistics and procurement, scholarship recipient**

I have worked with farmers and found out that they have challenges, such as crop diseases, poor yields... **Byakatonda Gerald, agricultural science and entrepreneurship, scholarship recipient**

I want to be an advocate and an activist for girl-child education, employment opportunities and human rights... — **Kalule Toney, social work and administration, scholarship recipient**

The UCU Sports Choir leads the university through a worship session at a Community Worship in Nkoyoyo Hall

The Rev. Eng. Paul Wasswa Ssembiro, the UCU Chaplain

CHAPLAINCY

Uganda Christian University offers on-site services with leadership from priests educated in biblical principles and practices. Services provided by the campus chaplaincy include Bible studies, spiritual counselling, chapel services throughout the week, and mission trips. Students have the opportunity not just to grow within their academic courses, but also to deepen their knowledge and faith in Christ under the guidance of a loving, caring ministerial staff.

Students can also participate as singers and musicians in Christian music, including some songs in the mother-tongue, as well as English.

UCU community during the Worship Hour in Nkoyoyo Hall

Rev. Dr. Stephen Noll, UCU's first Vice Chancellor

OTHER PROGRAMMES

Uganda Christian University (UCU) is continually adding faith, career and learning programmes and services to benefit students and staff. Among these are:

○ The Allan Galpin Health Centre – Offers clinical assessment and full-time medical doctor consultation.

○ The Career Development and Placement Office – Works with Alumni, Communications and Marketing, External Relations to advise students about employment possibilities.

○ African Policy Centre – Operates as a think-tank with a wide range of programming, including policy lecture series focused on promoting dialogue with Christian understanding on current issues, policy, and political thought.

○ Institute of Faith, Learning and Service – Provides guidance regarding integration of Christian teachings into curriculum and other UCU programmes.

○ The e-learning lab offers state-of-the-art technology for e-conferencing.

ACADEMIC STRUCTURE OF UCU

As of February 2020

Welcome to the Academic Structure of UCU

- Within Uganda Christian University, there are eight Faculties or Schools: Business and Administration, Education and Arts, Law, Science and Technology, the School of Medicine, Social Sciences, the Bishop Tucker School of Theology and Divinity, and Journalism, Communication & Media Studies. These faculties or schools are the major communities of scholars within a common disciplinary tradition that provide the first general structure of the academic offerings of the University.

- Within some of the Faculties or Schools, there are smaller units called departments. Examples of these are the department of Management and Entrepreneurship within the Business and Administration Faculty, the department of Social Work within the Social Sciences Faculty, and the department of Nursing affiliated with the School of Medicine. The departments are smaller, more specialized groups of scholars and academic offerings found in some of the Faculties.

- Each Faculty or School, and departments found within them, host Programmes that award educational credentials, such as diploma, bachelor degrees, or masters degrees. These are the Programmatic areas that students pursue in order to grow in wisdom, knowledge, and skills in a certain disciplinary tradition and to achieve a credential indicating their proficiency in said area. Some examples are: the Diploma in Entrepreneurship & Information Technology in the Faculty of Science and Technology, the Bachelor of Laws (LLB) in the Faculty of Law, and the Master of Arts in Literature (MLIT) in the Faculty of Education and Arts.

- Finally, each Programme has courses/course units, which are smaller topical, educational experiences based on a curriculum for students gathered together to learn under the tutelage of lecturers/tutors, visitors, and one another. Typically course/course units extend over one semester of study at the University. Some examples of courses/course units are: courses on sustainable peace within the Bachelor of Human Rights, Peace and Humanitarian Interventions (BHRP) in the Social Science Faculty, courses on African Theology within the Master of Divinity (MDIV) Programme in the Bishop Tucker School of Theology and Divinity, and courses on microbiology and epidemiology within the Bachelor of Environmental Science (BES) in the School of Medicine. Some programmes have short courses with an award of certificates for successful skill completion.

102 programmes approved by the National Council for Higher Education

Bishop Tucker School of Divinity and Theology
1. Bachelor of Child Development and Children's Ministry (BCDCM)
2. Bachelor of Divinity (BD)
3. Master of Arts in Child Development (MACD)
4. Master of Arts in Theology (MAT)
5. Master of Arts in Theology and Development (MATD)
6. Master of Arts in Theology and Healthcare Management (MATH)
7. Master of Arts in Theology (Focus on Transformational Urban Leadership) (MATU)
8. Master of Divinity (MDIV)
9. Doctor of Ministry (DMIN)
10. PhD in Theology (PHDT)

Email: *btucker@ucu.ac.ug*

Faculty of Business and Administration
1. Diploma in Business Administration (DBA)
2. Diploma in Procurement & Logistics Management (DPLM)
3. Diploma in Project Planning & Management (DMPP)
4. Bachelor of Business Administration (BBA)
5. Bachelor of Business Computing (BBC)
6. Bachelor of Development Economics (BDE)
7. Bachelor of Economics and Management (BEM)
8. Bachelor of Human Resource Management (BHRM)
9. Bachelor of Information and Administrative Management (BIAM)
10. Bachelor of International Business Management (BIBM)
11. Bachelor of Procurement & Logistics Management (BPLM)
12. Bachelor of Project Planning and Entrepreneurship (BEPP)
13. Bachelor of Science in Accounting and Finance (BSAF)
14. Bachelor of Science in Economics and Statistics (BSES)
15. Bachelor of Science in Oil and Gas Management (BOGM)
16. Postgraduate Diploma in Human Resource Management (PGD HRM)
17. Bachelor of Tourism & Hospitality Management (BOTHM)
18. Executive Master of Business Administration (EMBA)
19. Master of Arts in Organizational Leadership and Management (MAOL)
20. Master of Business Administration (MBA)
21. Master of Business Administration – Oil and Gas Management (MBAO)
22. Master of Science in Procurement and Supply Chain Management (M.sc PSCM)

Email: *business@ucu.ac.ug*

Faculty of Science and Technology
1. Diploma in Entrepreneurship & Information Technology (DEIT)
2. Bachelor of Agricultural Science and Entrepreneurship (BASE)
3. Bachelor of Aquaculture & Fisheries Management (BAFM)
4. Bachelor of Computational Science (BCS)
5. Bachelor of Electronics & Communication Science (BECS)
6. Bachelor of Environmental Science (BES)
7. Bachelor of Science in Agribusiness (BSAG)
8. Bachelor of Science in Civil and Environmental Engineering (BSCEE)
9. Bachelor of Science in Computer Science (BSCS)
10. Bachelor of Science in Construction Project Management (BSCPM)
11. Bachelor of Science in Food Science and Technology (BFST)
12. Bachelor of Science in Information Technology (BSIT)
13. Postgraduate Diploma in Water and Sanitation (PGDWATSAN)
14. Master of Information Technology (MIT)
15. Master of Science in Agribusiness and Entrepreneurship (MAG)
16. Master of Science in Agriculture and Rural Development (MARD)
17. Master of Science in Environmental Science by Research (MES)
18. Master of Science in Agriculture by Research (MSAR)
19. Master of Science in Water and Sanitation (MSWATSAN)

Email: *fost@ucu.ac.ug*

Faculty of Social Sciences
1. Diploma in Social Work and Social Administration (DSWASA)
2. Bachelor of Development & Social Entrepreneurship (BDSE)
3. Bachelor of Governance and International Relations (BGIR)
4. Bachelor of Human Rights, Peace and Humanitarian Intervention (BHRP)
5. Bachelor of Organization and Development Management (BODM)
6. Bachelor of Public Administration and Management (BPAM)
7. Bachelor of Social Work and Social Administration (BSWASA)
8. Master of Arts in Counseling Psychology (MACP)
9. Master of Development Monitoring and Evaluation (MDME)
10. Master of Development Studies (MDEV)
11. Master of Public Administration & Management (MPAM)
12. Master of Research and Public Policy (MRPP)
13. Master of Social Work (MSW)
14. Postgraduate Diploma in Development Monitoring and Evaluation (PGDME)
15. Postgraduate Diploma in Public Administration and Management (PGDPA)

Email: *socialsciences@ucu.ac.ug*

Programmes approved by the National Council for Higher Education

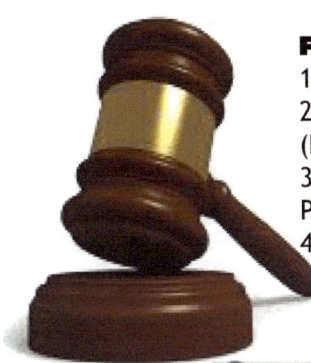

Faculty of Law
1. Bachelor of Laws (LLB)
2. Master of Laws in International Business Law (LLM-IBL)
3. Master of Laws in International Energy Law and Policy (LLM-IELP)
4. Master of Laws in Oil and Gas (LLM-OG)

Email: *law@ucu.ac.ug*

Faculty of Journalism, Communication & Media Studies
1. Bachelor of Arts in Mass Communication Journalism and Communication (BAMC)
2. Master of Arts in Journalism and Media Studies (MAJMS)
3. Master of Arts in Strategic Communication (MASC)

Email: *educationarts@ucu.ac.ug*

UCU School of Medicine
1. Diploma in Health Administration (DHA)
2. Diploma in Nursing (DNS)
3. Bachelor of Dental Surgery (BDS)
4. Bachelor of Environmental Health Science (BEHS)
5. Bachelor of Health Administration (BHA)
6. Bachelor of Medicine & Bachelor of Surgery (MBChB)
7. Bachelor of Nursing Science (BNS)
8. Bachelor of Public Health (BPH)
9. Bachelor of Science in Human Nutrition & Dietetics (BHND)
10. Master of Nursing Science (MNS)
11. Master of Public Health (MPH)
12. Master of Public Health Leadership-Save the Mothers (MPHL)
13. Master of Science in Human Nutrition (MSHN)

Email: *heathsciences@ucu.ac.ug*

Faculty of Education and Arts
1. Bachelor of Arts with Education (BAED)
2. Bachelor of Arts with Education - Fine Art Double Main (BAE-FA)
3. Bachelor of Arts in Languages (BAL)
4. Bachelor of Education (BED)
5. Bachelor of Industrial & Fine Art (BIFA)
6. Bachelor of Library and Information Science (BLIS)
7. Bachelor of Science with Education (BSED)
8. Master of Library and Information Science (MLIS)
9. Master of Arts in Literature (MLIT)
10. Master of Arts in Translation and Language Development (MATLD)
11. Master of Education in Planning and Administration (MEDAP)
12. Master of Human Resource Management in Education (MHRM)
13. PhD in Education Administration and Management (PEAM)
14. PhD in Literature (PhDL)
15. Postgraduate Diploma in Education (PGDE)
16. Postgraduate Diploma in Higher Education (PGDHE)

Email: *educationarts@ucu.ac.ug*

BISHOP TUCKER SCHOOL OF DIVINITY AND THEOLOGY

The Bishop Tucker Theological College was launched in 1913 to train Ugandan church leaders. In 1997, the College became Uganda Christian University, offering more disciplines for study.

The Bishop Tucker School of Divinity and Theology (BTSDT) is a community of full- and part-time students at the undergraduate and postgraduate levels.

Bishop Tucker School of Theology and Divinity exists to...

- Train men and women for pastoral and academic ministries through having the knowledge and love of God.
- Train them in godly living; Equip them to preach, evangelize, teach, and pastor in the knowledge and love of God throughout the world; and Serve the community of God's people.

The main disciplines offered are Theology, Divinity, and Child Ministry.

The School is headed by the Dean, Rev. Prof. Dr. Christopher Byaruhanga (BD, PGDE, CITS, ThD, PGDPL, PGDM) along with the Head of Department, Rev. Dr. Andrew David Omona (BA.ED/THEO, MA.Th, MA.IRD, PhD) in charge of Foundation Studies.

Programmes as of Feb. 2020
1. Bachelor of Child Development and Children's Ministry (BCDCM)
2. Bachelor of Divinity (BD)
3. Master of Arts in Child Development (MACD)
4. Master of Arts in Theology (MAT)
5. Master of Arts in Theology and Development (MATD)
6. Master of Arts in Theology and Healthcare Management (MATH)
7. Master of Arts in Theology (Focus on Transformational Urban Leadership) (MATU)
8. Master of Divinity (MDIV)
9. Doctor of Ministry (DMIN)
10. PhD in Theology (PHDT)

PROGRAMMES OVERVIEW

Bishop Tucker School of Divinity and Theology
Bachelor of Child Development and Children's Ministry (BCDCM)
Advent/September Intake – Full-time Day at Main/Mukono campus

Minimum Requirements
In addition to the other University admission requirements for undergraduate Programmes, one of the following categories will allow admission to this course:
- UACE certificate with at least 2 principal passes at the same sitting;
- Diploma in Child development, Social work, Education, Nursing, Theology and any other related field from a recognized institution of higher learning in any field or its equivalence;
- A Pass in mature-age examination administered by NCHE.

Programme Length
Three years, with maximum of five years to complete

Programme Highlights
Half of Uganda's population is under age 15. Globally and in East Africa, child abuse and neglect are growing concerns. The Bachelor of Child Development and Children's Ministry Programme equips students with the fundamentals of child development to counsel children and promote social protection and transformation of communities.

Courses
In addition to such foundational coursework, topics in the coursework within this Programme include, among others: Biblical theology of children, discipleship, special needs children, counseling, early childhood intervention and community development.

Career Prospects
This Programme prepares students for careers working with young children and their families. Students attain the skills to teach or direct child development Programmes, work as child development workers, probation and social welfare officers, developmental therapists, or in other areas of the early care and education field of children.

Bishop Tucker School of Divinity and Theology
Bachelor of Divinity (BD)
Trinity/May intake – Full-time Day at Mukono/Main campus

Minimum Requirement
In addition to the other University admission requirements for undergraduate Programmes, one of the following will allow admission to the course:
- Two principal passes at A' level, with at least 2 principal passes at same sitting;
- Diploma in theology from a recognized institution of higher learning;
- A Pass in mature-age examination administered by NCHE.
- All candidates must pass a faculty interview.

Programme Length
Three years, with maximum of five years to complete.

Programme Highlights
The Bachelor of Divinity Programme equips men and women to preach, evangelize, teach and care for God's people in knowledge and love of God. Content is delivered in lectures and practical training. In the final year, students complete a research project.

Courses
The more than 30 courses cover such topics as Christian worship, Old and New Testament, African traditional religion and Islam, pastoral care and counselling, world views, and the history and theology of the churches of the Anglican Communion, among others.

Career Prospects
Graduates will be prepared for multiple careers to serve God in church ministry and public life.

Bishop Tucker School of Divinity and Theology
Master of Arts in Child Development (MACD)
Advent/September Intake - Main/Mukono campus

Minimum Requirement
In addition to regular UCU requirements for postgraduate applicants, applicants need:
- Undergraduate degree or equivalent in child-related study such as education, child development, social work, community development, psychology and Christian ministry with a minimum of a second-class degree (2:2);
- Complete a faculty interview.

Programme Length
Two years with maximum of four years to complete dissertation

Programme Highlights
The Master of Arts in Child Development and Children's Ministry Programme addresses promoting children's literature and current issues for children, including those age 18 and younger with disabilities. The first year of the Programme focuses on seminars and dissertation writing is the focus in the second year.

Courses
Some topic in the course content includes, among others: adolescent development, child protection, management of child-focused organizations, writing for children, ministry to children with disabilities, child counseling and assessment and African Theology related to children.

Career Prospects
Career opportunities are related to a multi-disciplinary and holistic approach to designing and managing children's Programmes and projects in such organizations as UNICEF, Save the Children, Police Force, and Ministry of Labour, Gender and Social Welfare.

Bishop Tucker School of Theology and Divinity
Master of Arts in Theology and Development (MATD)
Trinity/May Intake - Modular at Mukono/Main campus

Minimum Requirement
In addition to regular UCU requirements and a commitment to human emancipation from a theological perspective, applicants need:
- Undergraduate degree or equivalent in divinity/theology, the humanities or other fields relevant to human service with a minimum of a second-class degree (2:2);
- Minimum two-years experience in ministry or service (parish, development, etc.)
- Pass a faculty interview.

Programme Length
Two years, with maximum of six years to complete

Programme Highlights
Focused on holistic development (Luke 4:18), particularly for those in spiritual, emotional and physical need, the Master of Arts in Theology and Development is designed to train faithful leaders with integrity and commitment who can contribute theologically infused reflection and practice of development Programmes and interventions.

Courses
Curriculum content within the Programme includes, among others: Biblical foundations of development, theology gender and development, Kiswahili, policy analysis, mentoring, evaluation, environment management in the church and non-profit management, among others.

Career Prospects
Those who successfully complete this Programme will be equipped with skills to assess problems, mobilize resources and address the structures and systems that perpetuate poverty and oppression in communities.

Bishop Tucker School of Theology and Divinity: Master of Arts in Theology (MAT)
Advent/September Intake - Distance learning with weekend classes; Trinity/May Intake - Modular at Mukono/Main campus

Minimum Requirement
Applicants should hold the following requirements:
- A Bachelor of Divinity or Bachelor of Arts in theology/religious studies or equivalent with at least a second-class degree (2:2);
- Pass a faculty interview.

Programme Length
Two years with maximum of four years to complete dissertation.

Programme Highlights
The Master of Arts in Theology is designed to equip men and women with added skills for pastoral academic ministry and research. Emphasis is on training in godly living to pastor people in the knowledge and love of God. This Programme has six specialization tracks: Biblical, Theological, Practical, Theoretical, Historical, Islam and Urban Leadership. Students select one of six tracks and take required courses in the Bible, Christian ethics and research methods.

Courses
Topical content in this course includes: interpreting the Bible from an African context, 21st century ethical and gender issues, Old and New Testament historical framework, Hebrew translation, global impact on churches in Africa, African mission practices, pastoral counselling, Christian-Muslim relations and Kiswahili language. Additional topics include counselling, expository preaching, gender issues, history and theology of ecumenism, new religious movements in Africa and Trinitarian and Christological controversies.

Career Prospects
Career prospects upon completing this degree can be found in local, national and international church and education sectors. Graduates will be equipped to be pastors, academic ministers, evangelists and teachers.

Bishop Tucker School of Theology and Divinity
Master of Arts in Theology and Health Care Management (MATH)
Trinity/May Intake - Full-time Day at Main/Mukono campus

Minimum Requirement
In addition to regular UCU requirements for postgraduate applicants, applicants need:
- Undergraduate degree or equivalent in divinity/theology, the humanities or other fields with a minimum of a second-class degree (2:2);
- Pass a faculty interview.

Programme Length
Two years, with maximum of four years to complete dissertation

Programme Highlights
With specific emphasis on HIV/AIDS, the Master of Arts in Theology and Health Care Management is characterized by one year of course work and one year of research and dissertation writing. With HIV/AIDS and related diseases a particular challenge in Africa, church leaders need to work alongside social workers and medical staff to provide pastoral care with counselling and Christian ethics. Instructors are experts in psychology, sociology, theology and health.

Courses
Curriculum content includes: African Bible interpretation, pastoral counselling, Christian healthcare practice, and the risk, impact, prevention and management of HIV/AIDS.

Career Prospects
Graduates will have knowledge and skills to formulate policy that takes religion, ethics and health issues into account, explain services to clients, facilitate community support and action, monitor HIV/AIDS prevention and care Programmes and demonstrate how health care management is part of the church mission.

Bishop Tucker School of Theology and Divinity
Master of Divinity (MDIV)
Trinity/May Intake - Full-time Day at Main/Mukono campus

Minimum Requirement
In addition to regular UCU requirements for postgraduate applicants, applicants need:
- Undergraduate degree or equivalent with a minimum of a second-class degree (2:2);
- Complete a faculty interview.

Programme Length
Three years with a maximum of six years to complete.

Programme Highlights
The Master of Divinity at Uganda Christian University focuses on the values and priorities of Jesus Christ while employing tools of quality Biblical and theology scholarship and engagement with subject-matter experts in the School. The first two years are grounded in coursework and third year focused on practical experience and individualized research.

Courses
The over two dozen courses cover such topics as: 21st century mission, Christian worship, counselling, African traditional religion and Islam, systematic theology, Biblical interpretation, evangelism and church leadership, management and finance. Hebrew and Greek are electives in this Programme.

Career Prospects
Graduates will be better prepared for ordained ministry as Christian leaders living, teaching and preaching the gospel.

Bishop Tucker School of Theology and Divinity
Master of Arts in Theology, Focus on Transformational Urban Leadership (MATU)
Easter/January Intake – Modular at Mukono/Main campus

Minimum Requirement
In addition to regular UCU requirements, the following are additional requirements for applicants:
- At least a second-class degree or its equivalent in Divinity/Theology, the humanities or any other fields relevant to human service;
- Minimum two years experience in ministry or service – parish, development work, or any field that gets one in contact with communities;
- Pass a faculty interview.
- Additionally, candidates should demonstrate a commitment to the goal of human emancipation from a theological perspective.

Programme Length
Two years, with maximum of four years to complete.

Programme Highlights
The course is designed for early- and mid-career professionals, including church workers and NGO employees, preparing for vocations in service among the world's urban poor. This urban leadership-focused Programme in theology is part of the social entrepreneurship field of study designed to meet the think-tank and action needs of the urban poor. The focus is on teaching management, character and mentoring skills to be used for empowerment of emergent, community leaders. Students will spend their first year engaged in coursework, and have their second year for research writing. In the first year, students will have three days of lectures and four days of practicum in slum contexts each week.

Courses
Topics in the coursework of the Programme include: ethics, urban movement, African languages, global theology, health care, counseling, community transformation, building faith communities and service among the marginalized, among others.

Career Prospects
Those who successfully complete this Programme will be equipped to transform and implement frameworks to improve life opportunities for informal (slum) settlement dwellers.

Bishop Tucker School of Theology and Divinity
PhD in Theology (PHDT)
Trinity/May Intake - Modular at Mukono/Main campus

Minimum Requirement
In addition to regular UCU requirements for postgraduate applicants, one of the following categories will allow admission to this course:
- Applicants need a master's degree in theology/Divinity, religious studies, or theology and development from a recognized institution of higher learning; or
- A Doctor of Ministry Degree from a recognized institution of higher learning;
- Additionally all applicants must submit a 20-30-page proposal for a dissertation (Candidates with a master's degree that did not require a dissertation may not qualify).

Programme Length
Three years, with maximum of six years to complete

Programme Highlights
The Doctor of Philosophy in Theology Programme is a highly specialized research degree offering opportunities to go deep into Christianity, theology, pastoral and biblical areas and within the social and political African context.

Courses
Curriculum content is delivered in nine graduate-level seminars with five in the major field and four in the minor field. Within the first year, there must be demonstrated competence in Greek, Hebrew or Swahili or other African language. Other offerings include: research methodology, African Biblical hermeneutics and Advanced Biblical theology. Research topics can come from such areas as Christianity in Africa, church and mission, historical theology, systematic theology, biblical studies, practical theology, theology and development, and African Christian theology, among others.

Career Prospects
This Programme prepares students for a vocation in theoretical instruction and Christian scholarly research and service for the church and society. Added research and writing skills improve critical and analytical engagement with contemporary African Christian issues to build the church and community.

Bishop Tucker School of Theology and Divinity
Doctor of Ministry (DMIN)
Trinity/May Intake - Modular at Mukono/Main campus

Minimum Requirement
In addition to regular UCU requirements for postgraduate applicants, applicants need:
- Applicants need a master's degree in theology, religious studies, and/or a Master of Divinity from a recognized institution of higher learning;
- All applicants must submit a 20-30-page proposal for a dissertation;

Programme Length
Three years, with maximum of six years to complete

Programme Highlights
Through a combination of academic study and experiences, students enrolled in the Doctor of Ministry in Mission Programme in the Bishop Tucker School of Theology and Divinity will be exposed to a variety of parish ministries, operations and best practices with emphasis on growth of holistic and godly communities.

Courses
Curriculum content in this Programme includes, among others: preaching, research, African Biblical theology, congregational development, pastoral care and counseling and mission trends.

Career Prospects
In addition to adding depth to current ministry positions and translating congregational development into real-life settings, graduates of this Programme will be qualified to teach at the university level.

In brief...

10
The number of programmes that the Bishop Tucker School of Theology and Divinity offers. Of these, two are undergraduate, the same number doctorate while the rest are master's

Duty
The school equips graduates with skills to preach, evangelize, teach, and pastor in the knowledge and love of God and to serve the community

20-30
All applicants for any of the two doctorate courses must submit a 20-30-page proposal for a dissertation as one of the minimum requirements

Bishop Tucker School of Divinity and Theology. [btucker@ucu.ac.ug]

FACULTY OF BUSINESS AND ADMINISTRATION

ABOUT THE FACULTY

The Faculty of Business and Administration started in 1997 as a Department of Business with 36 students. The Bachelor of Business Administration was the only undergraduate Programme offered in the department at the time. The faculty has since grown to three departments: Management and Entrepreneurship, Business and Finance, and the Economics and Statistics departments.

In 2014, Dr. Martin M. Lwanga(BA, MPA, MBA, D.BL) started as the Dean and Mr. Godfrey Sempungu (ICDL, DBE, BA.ED, MBA, M.Ph) is associate dean from 2016 to date. The faculty also has heads of department, Mrs. Elsie M. Nsiyona (Management & Entrepreneurship), Mr. Henry Mugisha (Business & Finance) and Mr. Peter Opio (Economics & Statistics).

FACULTY OF BUSINESS AND ADMINISTRATION

Programme list as of February 2020
1. Diploma in Business Administration (DBA)
2. Diploma in Procurement & Logistics Management (DPLM)
3. Diploma in Project Planning & Management (DMPP)
4. Bachelor of Business Administration (BBA)
5. Bachelor of Business Computing (BBC)
6. Bachelor of Development Economics (BDE)
7. Bachelor of Economics and Management (BEM)
8. Bachelor of Human Resource Management (BHRM)
9. Bachelor of Information and Administrative Management (BIAM)
10. Bachelor of International Business Management (BIBM)
11. Bachelor of Procurement & Logistics Management (BPLM)
12. Bachelor of Project Planning and Entrepreneurship (BEPP)
13. Bachelor of Science in Accounting and Finance (BSAF)
14. Bachelor of Science in Economics and Statistics (BSES)
15. Bachelor of Science in Oil and Gas Management (BOGM)
16. Bachelor of Tourism & Hospitality Management (BOTHM)
17. Post graduate diploma in Human Resource Management (PGD HRM)
18. Executive Master of Business Administration (EMBA)
19. Master of Arts in Organizational Leadership and Management (MAOL)
20. Master of Business Administration (MBA)
21. Master of Business Administration – Oil and Gas Management (MBAO)
22. Master of Science in Procurement and Supply Chain Management (M.SC PSCM)

PROGRAMMES OVERVIEW

Faculty of Business and Administration
Diploma of Business Administration (DBA)
Advent/September, Easter/January, Trinity/May Intakes - Full-time Day at Mukono/Main campus and Kampala campus

Minimum Requirement
Applicants for this Programme are required to have:
- Uganda Certificate of Education (UCE) or its equivalent;
- At least one principal pass and two subsidiary passes at A'level taken at the same sitting.

Programme Length
Two years, with maximum of four years to complete

Programme Highlights
The Diploma of Business Administration Programme focuses on a basic understanding of how the economy operates and is managed. The Diploma of Business Administration is meant to allow students to gain basic information about business administration, practical experience through internship opportunities, as well as e-learning options in the Programme. Through completing this diploma, the graduate will receive an exemption from the first years of the bachelor's degree in Business Administration and the upgrading can be done immediately after the students complete the diploma.

Courses
This Programme includes study in the following topics: business economics, business communications, business information technology, financial management, cost and management accounting, and principles of marketing, among others.

Career Prospects
Career prospects upon completing this degree can be found in local, national and international government, non-profit and private sectors with such titles as: accountants, finance assistants, marketers, audit assistants, and entrepreneurs.

Faculty of Business and Administration
Diploma in Procurement and Logistics Management (DPLM)
Advent/September, Easter/January, and Trinity May Intakes - Full-time Day at Mukono/Main campus and at Kampala campus.

Minimum requirement
Applicants are required to have:
- Uganda Certificate of Education (UCE) or its equivalent; and
- At least one principal pass and two subsidiary passes at A' level taken at the same sitting.

Programme length
Two years, with maximum of four years to complete

Programme Highlights
The Diploma in Procurement and Logistics Management aims to introduce students to the different facets of procurement and logistics management at diploma level. In additional to theory and practical skills, participants receive hands-on training in real-time procurement and emphasis on sustainability in relation to procurement.

Courses
Topical content in the Programme includes procurement, economics, warehouse and store management, supply chain management, marketing, accounting, strategic procurement, principles of procurement and supply chain management, international purchasing, quantitative methods, logistics, organizational behavior, and strategic procurement and supply chain management.

Careers
Among careers available for those who complete this Programme are managers of supply chain, fleet, stores; operations officers; procurement officers; and entrepreneurs.

Faculty of Business and Administration
Diploma in Project Planning and Management (DMPP)
Advent/September, Trinity/May and Easter/January - Full-time Day at Mukono/Main campus and at Kampala campus.

Minimum Requirement
Applicants are required to have:
- Uganda Certificate of Education (UCE) or its equivalent;
- At least one principal pass and two subsidiary passes at A' level taken at the same sitting.

Programme Length
Two years, with maximum of four years to complete

Programme Highlights
The Diploma in Project Planning and Management aims to build a solid educational foundation for all our diploma holders to work effectively in large complex projects and promote industry-wide standards for project management and educational maturity. This course will enable students appreciate the need for project integration, quality, and management of projects, including design, procurement, cost management and communication. Beyond this, the project also aims to equip graduates with knowledge of principles of management, human resource and strategic management of projects as well as human behavior in organizations

Courses
This Programme includes study in the following topics: monitoring and evaluation, project procurement management, strategic management, research methods, entrepreneurship and small business, project cost management and organizational behavior, among others.

Career Prospects
Career prospects upon completing the degree can be found in local, national and international government, non-profit and private sectors with such titles as: project manager, project officer, research assistant, or planning associate.

Faculty of Business and Administration [business@ucu.ac.ug]

Faculty of Business and Administration
Bachelor of Business Administration (BBA)

Advent/September, Easter/January, Trinity/May Intakes - Full-time Day and Evening at UCU-Mukono/Main campus and Kampala campus as well as at Mbale, Arua and Bishop Barham University College campuses.

Minimum Requirement
In addition to the other University admission requirements for undergraduate Programmes, one of the following categories will allow admission to this course:
- Direct entrants with the Uganda Certificate of Education (UCE) or its equivalent, and least 2 A' level advanced principal passes in Economics, Mathematics, Entrepreneurship and natural sciences taken in the same sitting;
- Diploma in Business Administration or related courses;
- A Pass in mature-age examination – such candidates must be Ugandan nationals of at least 25 years and have formal education. Those who are successful, in both the written and oral examination, are considered for admission.

Programme Length
Three years with maximum of five years to complete

Programme Highlights
The Bachelor of Business Administration in the Faculty of Business and Administration aims to expose students to the different facets of business in order to form well-qualified and thoughtful business professionals working from a strong Christian ethical framework. In the Programme, individualized learning and teamwork are emphasized with technical and relational curriculum relevant to real-world business opportunities, particularly in Uganda. A bachelor's degree in this Programme also lays the groundwork for master's degree studies.

Courses
Beyond foundational courses such as writing and study skills, and Old and New Testament, topical course content includes: marketing, entrepreneurship, business law, quantitative methods, statistics, accounting, auditing, taxation, public relations, international business, and consumer behaviour.

Career Prospects
Upon completing this degree, students are qualified to gain employment as accountants, financial advisers, marketers, commodities traders, loan officers, business managers, entrepreneurs of their own businesses and in real estate, and in human resource offices.

In brief...

22

The number of programmes in the Faculty of Business and Administration

BBA

Students getting this degree can become accountants, financial advisers, marketers, loan officers and more

Faculty of Business and Administration
Bachelor of Business Computing (BBC)

Advent/September Intake - Full-time Day at UCU-Mukono/Main campus

Minimum Requirement
In addition to the other University admission requirements for undergraduate Programmes, one of the following categories will allow admission to this course:
- Direct entrants with the Uganda Certificate of Education (UCE) or its equivalent, and least 2 A' level advanced passes in approved subjects taken at the same sitting;
- Holders of relevant diploma, in the desired field of study, from a recognized institution of higher learning;
- A Pass in mature-age examination – such candidates must be Ugandan nationals of at least 25 years and have formal education. Those who are successful, in both the written and oral examination, are considered for admission.

Programme Length
Three years, with maximum of five years to complete

Programme Highlights
In line with its mission of becoming the leading provider of quality business education as well as the increased use of computers in East African business operations and tasks, the Faculty of Business and Administration of Uganda Christian University developed a Bachelors of Business Computing (BBC) degree. This Programme provides students with the opportunity to acquire a thorough grounding in the fundamentals of computer science and core business and management skills while helping students reach the standard of knowledge and skills required by industry and professional bodies.

Courses
Topics within the courses in the Programme include: business Programmeming, discrete mathematics, marketing management, business economics, information systems, financial management, mobile applications development, computer networks, statistics, system analysis and design and business law.

Career Prospects
Career prospects upon completing this degree can be found in local, national and international government, non-profit and private sectors with such titles as: business/systems/technical/Programmer analyst, database administrator, intelligence/threat analyst, graphic designer, E-commerce project officer, Web developer, database administrator, and technical research officer.

Faculty of Business and Administration
Bachelor of Development Economics (BDE)
Advent/September Intake - Full-time Day at Mukono/Main Campus and Kampala campus and Arua Regional campus

Minimum Requirement
In addition to the other University admission requirements for undergraduate Programmes, one of the following categories will allow admission to this course:
- Diploma holders who studied a relevant course from a recognized institution of higher learning;
- Direct entrants who passed economics, math, entrepreneurship, and other subjects with two A' principal passes and must have passed mathematics at O' level taken in same sitting;
- A Pass in mature-age examination – such candidates must be Ugandan nationals of at least 25 years and have formal education. Those who are successful, in both the written and oral examination, are considered for admission.

Programme Length
Three years, with maximum of five years to complete

Programme Highlights
Rigorous understanding of how the economy operates, is formed and is managed is fundamental to governments, businesses, households, persons, and other institutions and organizations in the society. Graduates of the Bachelor of Development Economics in the Business and Administration Faculty will have a variety of knowledge and competencies in: modern economic theory, critical interpretation, understanding the enduring determinants of poverty, analysing the issues of fertility, education, health, work, migration and microfinance. This training is designed to allow students to understand how the economy relates to project of development in contemporary global contexts.

Courses
This Programme includes study in the following topics, among others: microeconomics, mathematical economics for development, labour market and development policy, credit market, entrepreneurship and development, international marketing for developing economies, and industrial structural development.

Career Prospects
Career prospects upon completing this degree can be found in local, national and international government, non-profit and private sectors with such titles as: research and development officers, Programme officers, economic analyst, as well as consultants.

Faculty of Business and Administration
Bachelor of Economics and Management (BEM)
Advent/September Intake - Full-time Day at UCU-Mukono/Main campus and Regional campuses

Minimum Requirement
In addition to the other University admission requirements for undergraduate Programmes, one of the following categories will allow admission to this course:
- Diploma holders who studied a relevant course from a recognized institution of higher learning;
- Direct entrants who passed economics, math, entrepreneurship, and other subjects with two A' principal passes and must have passed mathematics at O' level taken in the same sitting;
- A Pass in mature-age examination – such candidates must be Ugandan nationals of at least 25 years and have formal education. Those who are successful, in both the written and oral examination, are considered for admission.

Programme Length
Three years, with maximum of five years to complete

Programme Highlights
Rigorous understanding of how the economy operates and is managed is fundamental to governments, businesses, households, persons, and other institutions and organizations in the society. The Bachelor of Economics and Management Programme is designed to meet this need through training students in economic theory and management aspects that are relevant to understanding of how the economy works in contemporary global contexts.

Courses
This Programme includes coursework in the following topics: microeconomics, development economics, mathematical economics, political economy, organization and strategic planning management, econometrics, project planning, trade and negotiation and intellectual property, among others.

Career Prospects
Career prospects upon completing this degree can be found in local, national and international government, non-profit and private sectors with such titles as: research analyst, budget officer, loan officers, financial analyst, trader officer, credit officer, banking officer, sales analyst, insurance agent, Programme officer, planner, economist and consultant.

Faculty of Business and Administration
Bachelor of Business Administration (BBA)

Advent/September, Easter/January, Trinity/May Intakes - Full-time Day and Evening at UCU-Mukono/Main campus and Kampala campus as well as at Mbale, Arua and Bishop Barham University College campuses.

Minimum Requirement
In addition to the other University admission requirements for undergraduate Programmes, one of the following categories will allow admission to this course:
- Direct entrants with the Uganda Certificate of Education (UCE) or its equivalent, and least 2 A' level advanced principal passes in Economics, Mathematics, Entrepreneurship and natural sciences taken in the same sitting;
- Diploma in Business Administration or related courses;
- A Pass in mature-age examination – such candidates must be Ugandan nationals of at least 25 years and have formal education. Those who are successful, in both the written and oral examination, are considered for admission.

Programme Length
Three years with maximum of five years to complete

Programme Highlights
The Bachelor of Business Administration in the Faculty of Business and Administration aims to expose students to the different facets of business in order to form well-qualified and thoughtful business professionals working from a strong Christian ethical framework. In the Programme, individualized learning and teamwork are emphasized with technical and relational curriculum relevant to real-world business opportunities, particularly in Uganda. A bachelor's degree in this Programme also lays the groundwork for master's degree studies.

Courses
Beyond foundational courses such as writing and study skills, and Old and New Testament, topical course content includes: marketing, entrepreneurship, business law, quantitative methods, statistics, accounting, auditing, taxation, public relations, international business, and consumer behaviour.

Career Prospects
Upon completing this degree, students are qualified to gain employment as accountants, financial advisers, marketers, commodities traders, loan officers, business managers, entrepreneurs of their own businesses and in real estate, and in human resource offices.

In brief...

22
The number of programmes in the Faculty of Business and Administration

MBAO
The faculty, through the MBA - Oil and Gas Mgt wants to be a premier provider of petroleum and energy management education in East Africa.

Faculty of Business and Administration
Bachelor of Business Computing (BBC)

Advent/September Intake - Full-time Day at UCU-Mukono/Main campus

Minimum Requirement
In addition to the other University admission requirements for undergraduate Programmes, one of the following categories will allow admission to this course:
- Direct entrants with the Uganda Certificate of Education (UCE) or its equivalent, and least 2 A' level advanced passes in approved subjects taken at the same sitting;
- Holders of relevant diploma, in the desired field of study, from a recognized institution of higher learning;
- A Pass in mature-age examination – such candidates must be Ugandan nationals of at least 25 years and have formal education. Those who are successful, in both the written and oral examination, are considered for admission.

Programme Length
Three years, with maximum of five years to complete

Programme Highlights
In line with its mission of becoming the leading provider of quality business education as well as the increased use of computers in East African business operations and tasks, the Faculty of Business and Administration of Uganda Christian University developed a Bachelors of Business Computing (BBC) degree. This Programme provides students with the opportunity to acquire a thorough grounding in the fundamentals of computer science and core business and management skills while helping students reach the standard of knowledge and skills required by industry and professional bodies.

Courses
Topics within the courses in the Programme include: business Programmeming, discrete mathematics, marketing management, business economics, information systems, financial management, mobile applications development, computer networks, statistics, system analysis and design and business law.

Career Prospects
Career prospects upon completing this degree can be found in local, national and international government, non-profit and private sectors with such titles as: business/systems/technical/Programmer analyst, database administrator, intelligence/threat analyst, graphic designer, E-commerce project officer, Web developer, database administrator, and technical research officer.

Faculty of Business and Administration
Bachelor of Development Economics (BDE)
Advent/September Intake - Full-time Day at Mukono/Main Campus and Kampala campus and Arua Regional campus

Minimum Requirement
In addition to the other University admission requirements for undergraduate Programmes, one of the following categories will allow admission to this course:
• Diploma holders who studied a relevant course from a recognized institution of higher learning;
• Direct entrants who passed economics, math, entrepreneurship, and other subjects with two A' principal passes and must have passed mathematics at O' level taken in same sitting;
• A Pass in mature-age examination – such candidates must be Ugandan nationals of at least 25 years and have formal education. Those who are successful, in both the written and oral examination, are considered for admission.

Programme Length
Three years, with maximum of five years to complete

Programme Highlights
Rigorous understanding of how the economy operates, is formed and is managed is fundamental to governments, businesses, households, persons, and other institutions and organizations in the society. Graduates of the Bachelor of Development Economics in the Business and Administration Faculty will have a variety of knowledge and competencies in: modern economic theory, critical interpretation, understanding the enduring determinants of poverty, analysing the issues of fertility, education, health, work, migration and microfinance. This training is designed to allow students to understand how the economy relates to project of development in contemporary global contexts.

Courses
This Programme includes study in the following topics, among others: microeconomics, mathematical economics for development, labour market and development policy, credit market, entrepreneurship and development, international marketing for developing economies, and industrial structural development.

Career Prospects
Career prospects upon completing this degree can be found in local, national and international government, non-profit and private sectors with such titles as: research and development officers, Programme officers, economic analyst, as well as consultants.

Faculty of Business and Administration
Bachelor of Economics and Management (BEM)
Advent/September Intake - Full-time Day at UCU-Mukono/Main campus and Regional campuses

Minimum Requirement
In addition to the other University admission requirements for undergraduate Programmes, one of the following categories will allow admission to this course:
• Diploma holders who studied a relevant course from a recognized institution of higher learning;
• Direct entrants who passed economics, math, entrepreneurship, and other subjects with two A' principal passes and must have passed mathematics at O' level taken in the same sitting;
• A Pass in mature-age examination – such candidates must be Ugandan nationals of at least 25 years and have formal education. Those who are successful, in both the written and oral examination, are considered for admission.

Programme Length
Three years, with maximum of five years to complete

Programme Highlights
Rigorous understanding of how the economy operates and is managed is fundamental to governments, businesses, households, persons, and other institutions and organizations in the society. The Bachelor of Economics and Management Programme is designed to meet this need through training students in economic theory and management aspects that are relevant to understanding of how the economy works in contemporary global contexts.

Courses
This Programme includes coursework in the following topics: microeconomics, development economics, mathematical economics, political economy, organization and strategic planning management, econometrics, project planning, trade and negotiation and intellectual property, among others.

Career Prospects
Career prospects upon completing this degree can be found in local, national and international government, non-profit and private sectors with such titles as: research analyst, budget officer, loan officers, financial analyst, trader officer, credit officer, banking officer, sales analyst, insurance agent, Programme officer, planner, economist and consultant.

Faculty of Business and Administration
Bachelor of Human Resource Management (BHRM)
Advent/September Intake - Full-time Day at Mukono/Main campus and Day and Evening at Kampala campus

Minimum Requirement
In addition to the other University admission requirements for undergraduate Programmes, one of the following categories will allow admission to this course:
- Uganda Certificate of Education (UCE) or its equivalent and least 2 A' level principal passes taken in the same sitting;
- Relevant diploma, in a relevant field of study, from a recognized institution of higher learning;
- A Pass in mature-age examination – such candidates must be Ugandan nationals of at least 25 years and have formal education. Those who are successful, in both the written and oral examination, are considered for admission.

Programme Length
Three years, with maximum of five years to complete

Programme Highlights
The Bachelor of Human Resource Management Programme in the Faculty of Business and Administration emphasizes ethical recruitment, development, and management of people. Included topics within the Programme are communication and business decision-making, as well as orientation, training, and proper exit of employees. The curriculum is designed to produce honest, innovative and self-reliant human resource managers at various levels in an organization.

Courses
Individual courses within the Programme address such topics as basic marketing, accounting, computing; business law, health and safety, behavioral and operational management, strategic planning, and interpersonal relations, among others.

Career Prospects
Upon completing this degree, graduates will be equipped to work in local, national and international public and private institution human resource departments and become human resource managers.

Faculty of Business and Administration
Bachelor of Information and Administrative Management (BIAM)
Advent/September Intake - Full-time Day at Mukono/Main campus and Kampala campus

Minimum Requirements
In addition to the other University admission requirements for undergraduate Programmes, one of the following categories will allow admission to this course:
- Direct entrants with the Uganda Certificate of Education (UCE) or its equivalent and least 2 A' level principal passes taken in the same sitting; and/or
- Holders of a relevant diploma, in a relevant field of study, from a recognized institution of higher learning; and/or
- A Pass in mature-age examination – such candidates must be Ugandan nationals of at least 25 years and have formal education. Those who are successful, in both the written and oral examination, are considered for admission.

Programme Length
Three years, with maximum of five years to complete

Programme Highlights
The Bachelor of Information and Administrative Management at is aligned with the faculty of Business and Administration's mission of becoming the leading provider of quality business education to the people in Uganda and the region and as well as the need for highly skill administrators and managers. This Programme is designed to develop a cadre of professionals with integrity, power of critical enquiry, logical thought, and wise judgment in a Christian perspective to perform with excellence in managerial, information and administrative roles.

Courses
Topics in the coursework of the Programme include: business economics, principles of management, fundamentals of accounting, office organization and management, social administration, public relations and customer care, human resource management, records management, administrative law, industrial psychology, and public administration, among others.

Career Prospects
Career prospects upon completing this degree can be found in local, national and international government, non-profit and private sectors with such titles as: administrative secretaries, public administrators, record managers, office managers, executive officers, personal assistants, and executive secretaries.

Faculty of Business and Administration
Bachelor of Tourism and Hospitality Management (BOTHM)
Advent/September Intake - Full-time Day at Mukono/Main campus

Minimum Requirement
In addition to the other University admission requirements for undergraduate Programmes, one of the following categories will allow admission to this course:
- Uganda Certificate of Education (UCE) or its equivalent and least 2 A' level principal passes taken in the same sitting;
- Relevant diploma, in a relevant field of study, from a recognized institution of higher learning;
- A Pass in mature-age examination – such candidates must be Ugandan nationals of at least 25 years and have formal education. Those who are successful, in both the written and oral examination, are considered for admission.

Programme Length
Three years, with five years to completion

Programme Highlights
The Bachelor of Tourism and Hospitality Management in the Faculty of Business and Administration focuses on preparing graduates for serving others in leisure, entertainment, and culinary industries. Critical Thinking, problem-solving skills, and the ability to work in a team will be emphasized along with Christian principles, including moral and ethical behavior in light of the life of Christ.

Students during a hospitality management practical lesson

Courses
Among the more than 40 courses leading to this degree Programme are those dealing with plants and wildlife, promotion, food management, convention and concert planning and accommodation.

Career Prospects
Graduates of this Programme will be qualified for serving in their own businesses or working in other hospitality industries such as national parks and hotels. Possible jobs are related to hospitality, tour, catering, and events. Possible positions are customer hospitality manager, relationship manager, tourism resource planner, and safari tour guide, among others.

Faculty of Business and Administration
Bachelor of International Business and Management (BIBM)
Advent/September Intake - Full-time Day at UCU-Mukono/Main campus

Minimum Requirement
In addition to the other University admission requirements for graduate Programmes, one of the following categories will allow admission to this course:
- Direct entrants with the Uganda Certificate of Education (UCE) or its equivalent and least 2 A' level advanced principle passes taken at the same sitting; and/or
- Diploma from a recognised institution of Higher Learning; or
- A Pass in mature-age examination – such candidates must be Ugandan nationals of at least 25 years and have formal education. Those who are successful, in both the written and oral examination, are considered for admission.

Programme Length
Three years, with maximum of five years to complete.

Programme Highlights
The Bachelor of International Business and Management is aligned with the Business and Administration faculty's mission of becoming the leading provider of quality business education in the Ugandan region and the drive towards regional integration and increased business globalization. The Programme is designed to develop a cadre of professionals with integrity, power of critical enquiry, logical thought, and wise judgment in a Christian perspective for essential knowledge and skills in ethical decision making in the international business environment.

Courses
Topics in the coursework of the Programme include: business economics, accounting fundamentals, marketing management, international management, business law, international trade, entrepreneurship, strategic planning, world cultures and business, and global supply chain management, among others.

Career Prospects
Career prospects upon completing this degree can be found in local, national and international government, non-profit and private sectors with such titles as: accountant, consultant, financial analyst, human resource officer, marketing managers and corporate buyers.

The Bachelor of International Business and Management is designed to develop a cadre of professionals with integrity, power of critical enquiry, logical thought, and wise judgment in a Christian perspective for essential knowledge and skills in ethical decision making in the international business environment

Faculty of Business and Administration
Bachelor of Project Planning and Entrepreneurship (BEPP)
Advent/September Intake - Full-time Day at Mukono/Main campus and Evening at Kampala campus

Minimum Requirement
In addition to the other University admission requirements for undergraduate Programmes, one of the following categories will allow admission to this course:
- Diploma holders who studied a relevant course from a recognized institution of higher learning;
- Direct entrants who passed economics, math, entrepreneurship, and other subjects with two A' principal passes and must have passed mathematics at O' level taken in the same sitting;
- A Pass in mature-age examination – such candidates must be Ugandan nationals of at least 25 years and have formal education. Those who are successful, in both the written and oral examination, are considered for admission.

Programme Length
Three years, with maximum of five years to complete

Programme Highlights
The Bachelor of Project Planning and Entrepreneurship in the Faculty of Business and Administration aims to expose students to different facets of Project Planning and Entrepreneurship. Throughout the Programme, entrepreneurship is emphasised with the realization of its role to growth of national economies. Particularly, the International Labour Organization (ILO) and Student Entrepreneurship Programme (STEP) models are applied in a curriculum that includes theory and practical aspects of starting and operating a business.

Courses
Individual courses address various business-related topics including: finance, law, technology, customer relations, project management, personnel management and competition, among other topics.

Career Prospects
Upon completing this degree, graduates will be equipped to implement projects, start their own businesses and help current businesses grow.

Faculty of Business and Administration
Bachelor of Science in Accounting and Finance (BSAF)
Advent/September and Trinity/May Intake - Full-time Day at Mukono/Main campus and Kampala campus

Minimum Requirement
In addition to the other University admission requirements for undergraduate Programmes, one of the following categories will allow admission to this course:
- Direct entrants with the Uganda Certificate of Education (UCE) or its equivalent, and least 2 A' level principal passes in Mathematics, Economics or Entrepreneurship taken at the same sitting. For Arts subjects, a student must have obtained a credit in Mathematics at O-level;
- A diploma in Accounting and Finance or any other related qualification;
- A Pass in mature-age examination – such candidates must be Ugandan nationals of at least 25 years and have formal education. Those who are successful, in both the written and oral examination, are considered for admission.

Programme Length
Three years, with maximum of five years to complete.

Programme Highlights
The Bachelor of Science in Accounting and Finance in the Faculty of Business and Administration aims to provide rigorous study of accounting and finance. The Programme has a strong vocational orientation that prepares students to progress in such certifications as Certified Public Accountant (CPA), Association of Chartered Certified Accountants (ACCA), and Certified Investment Management Analyst (CIMA).

Courses
In addition to such foundation courses as communications and the Bible, topics in the coursework include: marketing, quantitative methods, human resource management, organizational behaviour and analysis, tax theory and policy, accounting, entrepreneurship, and strategic management, among others.

Career Prospects
Graduates of the BSAF Programme could pursue careers and become accountants, financial advisors, auditor, banking, and insurance and business consultants.

Faculty of Business and Administration
Bachelor of Science in Economics and Statistics (BSES)
Advent/September and Trinity/May Intakes - Full-time Day at Mukono/Main campus and Mbale regional campuses

Minimum Requirements
In addition to the other University admission requirements for undergraduate Programmes, one of the following categories will allow admission to this course:
- Diploma holders who studied a relevant course from a recognized institution of higher learning;
- Direct entrants who passed economics, mathematics, and other subjects with two A' principal passes and must have passed mathematics at O' level taken in the same sitting;
- A Pass in mature-age examination – such candidates must be Ugandan nationals of at least 25 years and have formal education. Those who are successful, in both the written and oral examination, are considered for admission.

Programme Length
Three years, with maximum of five years to complete

Programme Highlights
Much management work around the world involves measurement in numbers – quantitative data. Students in the Bachelor of Science in Economics and Statistics in the Faculty of Business and Administration at Uganda Christian University receive economic and statistical knowledge and skill to analyse issues and communicate results orally and in writing. Christian values and ethics are reinforced throughout the Programme in order to form economics and statistics professionals who have a strong Christian foundation for their work.

Courses
In addition to foundational courses in such areas as writing skills and the Old Testament and the New Testament teachings, topics within this Programme's courses include, among others: mathematical economics, microeconomics, statistical data modeling, probability theory, multivariate analysis and agricultural, monetary and labour economics.

Career Prospects
Graduates of this Programme can find career opportunities in non-profit, public and provide institutions. Positions include research/monitoring/evaluation officers, district planners, biostatisticians, consultants, Programme officers, economic/financial/sales analysts, loan officers and insurance agents.

Faculty of Business and Administration
Bachelor of Science Oil and Gas Management (BOGM)
Advent/September Intake - Full-time Day at Institute of Petroleum Studies, Kampala.

Minimum requirement
Applicants for this Programme must have:
- Uganda Certificate of Education (UCE) or its equivalent with at least 2 A' level advanced passes in one of Economics, Arts, Entrepreneurship, and Natural Sciences taken at the same sitting.

Programme length
Three years, with maximum of five years to complete

Programme Highlights
The BSc. Oil & Gas Management Programme sponsored through the Faculty of Business and Administration lays the foundation for sound reasoning in Oil and Gas industry. Students are given a stepping stone into the rapidly changing and stimulating world of energy exploration, oil and gas project management, and the marketing, organization and retailing of products concerned with the extractive industries. In Uganda, at the moment, there are numerous companies involved in up-stream and down-stream operations with consultants, transporters and transfer specialists, maintenance companies, retailers, etc. and a graduate of this Programme would be well positioned to work in various sectors of the industry.

Courses
Topics in the coursework include: principles of marketing, business law, oil and gas management, marketing management, international energy policies, business economics, legal aspects of the oil and gas industry, production and operations management, taxation management.

Career Prospects
Among careers available for those who complete this Programme are consultants, transporters and transfer specialists, retailers, legal officers in oil and gas, and managers of petroleum companies.

Faculty of Business and Administration
Bachelors in Procurement and Logistics Management (BPLM)
Advent/September Intake - Full-time Day at UCU-Mukono (Main) campus and at Kampala campus; Trinity/May Intake - Full-time Day at UCU-Mukono (Main) campus and at Kampala campus

Minimum requirement
In addition to the other University admission requirements for undergraduate Programmes, one of the following categories will allow admission to this course:
- Direct entrants with the Uganda Certificate of Education (UCE) or its equivalent and least 2 A' level principal passes taken in the same sitting; and/or
- Holders of a relevant diploma, in a relevant field of study, from a recognized institution of higher learning; and/or
- A Pass in mature-age examination – such candidates must be Ugandan nationals of at least 25 years and have formal education. Those who are successful, in both the written and oral examination, are considered for admission.

Programme length
Three years, with maximum of five years to complete

Programme Highlights
The Bachelors in Procurement and Logistics Management in the Faculty of Business and Administration aims to teach students to understand the different facets of procurement and logistics management. In additional to theory and practical skills, participants in this course receive hands-on training in real-time procurement and emphasis on sustainability in relation to logistics.

Courses
Topics in the coursework include, among others: procurement, economics, warehouse and store management, supply chain management, marketing, accounting, strategic procurement, relationship management, quantitative methods, logistics, organizational behavior and contract management.

Career Prospects
Among careers available for those who complete this Programme are managers of supply chain, fleet, stores, and operations; procurement officers; and entrepreneurs.

In brief...

25

In order to qualify for admission for the Bachelors in Procurement and Logistics Management Programme, a person must be Ugandan nationals of at least 25 years and have formal education

Oil & Gas

The Bachelor of Science Oil and Gas Management gives students a stepping stone into the rapidly changing and stimulating world of energy exploration, oil and gas project management

Faculty of Business and Administration
Post graduate Diploma in Human Resource Management

Advent/September Intake - Weekend at Kampala Campus

Minimum Requirement
To qualify for admission to this Programme, beyond all other normal graduate Programme requirements, the candidate must:
• At least have an honours degree or its equivalent in any developmental discipline (Social Sciences, Humanities, Physical sciences, Business and Management sciences) from a recognized University.

Programme Length
One year, maximum two years to complete

Programme Highlights
The Postgraduate Diploma in Human Resource Management is a Programme designed to train and equip students with leadership and management skills, theories and concepts of human resource management with high standard of integrity, professionalism and high moral standards.

Courses
This course includes study in the following areas, among others: Human Resource Management, Christian Philosophy and Social Ethics, Management Information Systems, Financial Management for HR, Administrative and Labor Law, Strategic Management and Planning, and Training and Development.

Career Prospects
Career prospects upon completing this degree can be found in local, national and international government, non-profit and private sectors with such titles as: Human Resource Manager, Human Resource Officer, Head of HR Compliance, HR Assistant, HR Training and Development.

Columbus State Community College President, Dr. David Harrison, networks with UCU Business Faculty Dean, Dr. Martin Lwanga

Faculty of Business and Administration
Master of Arts in Organizational Leadership (MAOL)
Advent/September Intake - Distance Learning with one-week residency on Mukono campus every six months

Minimum Requirement
To qualify for admission to this Programme, beyond the normal graduate Programme requirements, the candidate must:
- Have organizational management experience;
- Applicants need to have an undergraduate degree from a recognized university with a minimum second lower (2:2).

Programme Length
Three years, with maximum of five years to complete

Programme Highlights
The Master of Arts in Organizational Leadership and Management Programme in the Faculty of Business and Administration focuses on knowledge and skills from business in light of Christian principles, through individual research, professor guidance and peer-to-peer engagement. Emphasis is on application of principles to everyday work.

Courses
Content in the coursework includes, among others: servant and women's leadership, impact of teaching and learning, strategic management, integrity and finance, research methodology, spiritual formation, conflict management, ethical living and leadership, fundraising, partnerships and development.

Career Prospects
Career prospects upon completing this degree can be found in local, national and international government, church, non-profit and private sectors with such titles as: finance manager, human resource manager, organizational strategist, culture and diversity specialist, development and social change specialist, conflict management, transformation consultant, and adult learning specialist.

In brief...

MAOL
The The Master of Arts in Organizational Leadership and Management Programme focuses on knowledge and skills through individual research, professor guidance and peer-to-peer engagement

EMBA
The Executive Master of Business Administration Programme provides training for people of substantial competency in management and business administration skills

UCU Faculty of Business and Administration
Executive Master of Business Administration (EMBA)
Advent/September Intake - Weekend at Kampala Campus

Minimum Requirement
To qualify for admission to this Programme, beyond all other normal graduate Programme requirements, the candidate must:
- Have business/organizational management experience, whether in the public or private sector, for at least two years at middle or top management level;
- Applicants need to have an undergraduate degree from a recognized university with a minimum second lower (2:2);
- Complete the University Administered Graduate Management Admission (GMAT) Test with a pass mark of 60%.

Programme Length
Two years, including the research project

Programme Highlights
The Executive Master of Business Administration Programme in the Faculty of Business and Administration provides quality training for people of substantial competency and interest in management and business administration skills. The Programme is highly flexible with the aim of helping senior managers from various backgrounds and representing a wide variety of organizations and industries to increase their qualification. The Participant-Centred Learning approach is used as a mode of teaching as well as a focus on case study methodology in every course unit.

Courses
This course includes study in the following areas, among others: management theory and practice, accounting and finance for managers, business ethics, strategic marketing management, organizational behaviour, project planning, and business/company law.

Career Prospects
Career prospects upon completing this degree can be found in local, national and international government, non-profit and private sectors with such titles as: business advisor, business manager, consultant, policy analyst, and technical specialist.

Faculty of Business and Administration
Masters of Business Administration (MBA)
Advent/September Intake - Weekend at UCU-Kampala campus and Easter/January - Weekend at Mukono/Main campus

Minimum Requirement
In addition to the other University admission requirements for graduate Programmes, to qualify for admission to this Programme the candidate must:
- Have an undergraduate degree with a minimum second lower (2:2) from a recognized university; or
- Applicants without a second lower (2:2) are required to complete a Postgraduate Diploma in Business Administration;
- Complete a University administrated Graduate Management Admission Test (GMAT) with a pass mark of 60%.

Programme Length
Two years, with maximum of four years to complete.

Programme Highlights
In line with its mission of becoming the leading provider of quality business education to the people in Uganda and the region, the Faculty of Business and Administration at Uganda Christian University started a Master's degree in Business Administration. This Programme is designed to provide advanced training for people of substantial competency and keen interest in the discipline of management and business administration and research methodologies. These areas are central for managing profitably and sustaining firms, gaining a firm understanding of the broad intellectual tradition of business management and administration, and being able to conduct excellent scientific research in business management and administration.

Courses
Coursework in the Programme includes, among others: management theory and practice, financial and management accounting, corporate governance, advanced project planning and management, business and company law, monitoring and evaluation, and business and company law.

Career Prospects
Career prospects upon completing this degree can be found in local, national and international government, non-profit and private sectors with such titles as: accountant, business manager, corporate recruiter, finance officer, financial manager, financial analyst, human resource manager, management analyst, management consultant, and research analyst.

TO APPLY...
www.ucu.ac.ug/academics/master-of-business-administration

Faculty of Business and Administration
Master of Business Administration – Oil and Gas Management (MBAO)
Advent/September and Easter/January intakes - Weekend at Institute of Petroleum Studies Kampala.

Minimum Requirement
To qualify for admission to this Programme and in addition to all normal graduate Programme requirements, the candidate must:
- Possess an undergraduate degree with a minimum second lower (2:2) from a recognized university.

Programme Length
Two years, including the research project

Programme Highlights
The Faculty of Business and Administration is positioning itself to be one of the premier providers of Petroleum and Energy Management Education in East Africa. The Master of Business Administration – Oil and Gas Management Programme aims to train learners to apply knowledge and skills gained in the Programme to enhance their administrative and managerial effectiveness in the oil and gas sector through a highly interactive, market-oriented learning environment based on global academic standards and Christian values.

Courses
This Programme includes study in the following areas, among others: global oil and gas, business ethics, financial and management accounting, oil and gas law, business policy in oil and gas, and supply chain management.

Career Prospects
Career prospects upon completing this degree can be found in local, national and international government, non-profit and private sectors with such titles as: advisor, manager, consultant, policy analyst and technical specialist.

2:2

All the master's programmes in the Faculty of Business and Administration require the applicant to have attained a an undergraduate degree from a recognized university with a minimum second lower (2:2)

Faculty of Business and Administration
Master of Science in Procurement and Supply Chain Management (M.SC PSCM)
Trinity/May/ Intake – Evening Weekend at Kampala Campus

Minimum Requirement
To qualify for admission to this Programme, beyond all other normal graduate Programme requirements, the candidate must:
- Have an undergraduate degree from a recognized university with a minimum second lower (2:2);

Programme Length
Two years, including the research project

Programme Highlights
The Master of Science in Procurement and Supply Chain Management Programme in the Faculty of Business and Administration provides quality training for people of substantial competency and interest in procurement. The Programme is highly flexible with the aim of helping senior managers, heads of department, procurement management, project leaders, and various professionals in leadership positions to increase their qualification. The Programme also is useful to fresh graduates who want to make a career in Procurement and Supply Chain Management. On completion of coursework and lectures, a student will be eligible for Post Graduate Diploma in Procurement and Supply Chain Management.

Courses
This course includes study in the following areas, among others: sustainable and ethical procurement, supply chain risk management, Information Systems, procurement law, supply chain operations and modeling, strategic supply chain management, negotiations and contract management.

Career Prospects
Career prospects upon completing this degree can be found in local, national and international government, non-profit and private sectors with such titles as: procurement manager, officer, assistant; clearing and forwarding manager; supply chain manager; and store manager.

FACULTY OF EDUCATION AND ARTS

ABOUT THIS FACULTY

The Faculty of Education and Arts since its inception in 1997 has trained and continues to train a cadre of Education and Arts professionals with Christian values. The faculty offers courses in Education, Languages and Literature at both Undergraduate and Postgraduate levels.

The faculty is headed by the Dean, Dr. Richard Watuulo (B.ED, MA, PhD) along with Heads of Department. Mr. Joel Masagazi Yaawe (Education), Dr. Constance Tukwasibwe (Languages and Literature), Dr. William Kayamba (Industrial and Fine Art) and Dr. Sarah Kaddu (Library Studies).

FACULTY OF EDUCATION AND ARTS

Programme list as of February 2020
1. Bachelor of Arts with Education (BAED)
2. Bachelor of Arts with Education - Fine Art Double Main (BAE-FA)
3. Bachelor of Arts in Languages (BAL)
4. Bachelor of Education (BED Primary)
5. Bachelor of Education (BED Secondary)
6. Bachelor of Industrial & Fine Art (BIFA)
7. Bachelor of Library and Information Science (BLIS)
8. Bachelor of Science with Education (BSED)
9. Master of Library and Information Science (MLIS)
10. Master of Arts in Literature (MLIT)
11. Master of Arts in Translation and Language Development (MATLD)
12. Master of Education, Planning and Administration (MEDAP)
13. Master of Human Resource Management in Education (MHRM)
14. PhD in Education Administration and Management (PEAM)
15. PhD in Literature (PhDL)
16. Postgraduate Diploma in Education (PGDE)
17. Postgraduate Diploma in Higher Education (PGDHE)

PROGRAMMES OVERVIEW

Faculty of Education and Arts
Department of Education
Bachelor of Arts with Education (BAED)
Advent/September Intake – Full-time Day at Main/Mukono campus

Minimum Requirement
In addition to overall university requirements for degree Programme entry, applicants for this Programme must:
• Hold at least the Uganda Advanced Certificate of Education (UACE) or its equivalent with at least two principal passes in subjects related to their choice for major, obtained in the same sitting.

Programme Length
Three years minimum and five years maximum to finish

Programme Highlights
The Bachelor of Arts with Education Programme in the Faculty of Education and Arts is de-signed to enable students explore knowledge in their areas of specialty that could be a combination of religion and history, communications and geography and English and litera-ture, among other combinations as indicated below. Students will develop mastery of their area of specialization and learn to communicate effectively, handle secondary school stu-dents with discipline, and act as role models to promote Christian spiritual and moral for-mation.

Subject Combinations
• ART DM, ENG DM (ENG/LIT), COM/CRE, COM/GEO, CRE/GEO, CRE/HIST, ECO/CRE, ECO/GEO, HIST/COM, HIST/CRE, HIST/ECO, HIST/GEO, HIST/KIS, HIST/LUG, KIS/CRE.

Career Prospects
Graduates of this Programme are ready to start a career as professional teachers and education service providers.

Faculty of Education and Arts
Bachelor of Arts with Education (Fine Art Double Main) (BAE-FA)
Advent/September and Trinity/May Intakes – Full-time Day Mukono/Main campus, and also Bishop Barham University College, Mbale University, and Arua campuses

Minimum Requirement
In addition to the other University admission requirements for undergraduate Programmes, one of the following categories will allow admission to this course:
• Hold Advanced level qualifications with principle pass in Fine Art;
• Diploma in art-related courses.

Programme Length
Three years, with maximum of five years to complete

Programme Highlights
Recognizing East Africa's rich, artistic cultural background, the Bachelor of Arts with Edu-cation (Fine Art Double Main) Programme is designed to maximize the creativity and inde-pendent thinking of students while providing context and structure to various art forms. In addition to structured curriculum, students will have opportunities for art shows on and off campus.

Courses
Topics in the content of the coursework, beyond foundational courses such as writing and study skills, and Old and New Testament include, among others: computer graphics, draw-ing, painting, clay modeling, ceramics, sculpture, use of fabrics, art teaching methods, and the art of ancient and modern world, East African contemporary art, and European middle ages and late gothic age.

Career Prospects
Upon completing this degree, students are qualified to teach Art at the secondary level as well as become graphic and costume designers and art entrepreneurs in various mediums.

Faculty of Education and Arts

Department of Languages and Literature
Bachelor of Arts in Languages (BAL)
Advent/September Intake – Full-time Day at Main/Mukono campus

Minimum Requirement
In addition to overall university requirements for degree Programme entry, applicants for this Programme must:
- Hold at least the Uganda Advanced Certificate of Education (UACE) or its equivalent with at least two principle passes in subjects related to their choice for major, obtained in the same sitting.

Programme Length
Three years, with five years maximum to finish

Programme Highlights
The Bachelor of Arts in Languages Programme in the Faculty of Education and Arts is designed to enable students to explore linguistic knowledge and abilities in their areas of specialty, within the languages of Kiswahili, French, and German. Other languages may be available in consultation with the Faculty. Students will develop mastery of their area of specialization and learn to communicate effectively, handle secondary school students with discipline, and act as role models to promote Christian spiritual and moral formation.

Subject Combinations
Kiswahili, French, German

Career Prospects
Graduates of this Programme are ready to start a career as professional teachers, journalists, translators, and education service providers.

Faculty of Education and Arts

Department of Education
Bachelor of Education (BED)
Easter/January Intake – Modular at Main/Mukono campus as well as Mbale University College, Bishop Barham University College, Arua campuses

Minimum Requirement
In addition to overall university requirements for degree Programme entry, applicants for this Programme must:
- Have Diploma in Secondary Education of at least lower second class. The student has to study the subjects he or she offered at diploma level.

Programme Length
Two years minimum and four years maximum to finish

Programme Highlights
This Programme is meant for training secondary school teachers who are diploma holders who are interested in upgrading their degree level. It is a convenient teacher friendly modular holiday Programme comprising six modules covered in two years. This Programme offers an in service opportunity for continuing professional training and development for secondary school teachers. The Programme is meant to help them upgrade thus improve on their knowledge, skills and attitudes/values, in order to offer better teaching services.

Subject Combinations
- The student has to study the subjects he or she offered at diploma level.

Career Prospects
Graduates of this Programme are ready to advance in a career as professional teachers and education service providers.

Faculty of Education and Arts

Bachelor of Industrial and Fine Art (BIFA)
Advent/September and Trinity/May Intakes - Full-Time Day Mukono/Main campus, as well as Bishop Barham University College, Mbale University, Arua campuses

Minimum Requirements
In addition to the other University admission requirements for undergraduate Programmes, one of the following categories will allow admission to this course:
- Advanced level qualifications with at least two principal passes obtained at the same sitting with one principal pass C in fine art;
- Diploma in art-related courses.

Programme Length
Three years with a maximum of five years to complete

Programme Highlights
Art requires aesthetic, intellectual and practical skills. The Bachelor of Industrial and Fine Art Programme builds these skills and combines these skills with industry by connections in such areas as studio art, industrial design, and gallery management.

Courses
Topics in the content of the coursework include, among others: drawing, sculpture, paint-ing, fabric design and decoration, computer graphics, ceramics, intermediate computer graphics, fashion and interior design, armature construction, and imaginative and exag-gerative drawing.

Career Prospects
Upon completing this degree, students are qualified to teach fine art at the secondary school level, work in fabric factories as designers and operate independent art galleries.

Faculty of Education and Arts
Department of Library and information Science
Bachelor of Library and Information Science (BLIS)
Advent/September Intake - Full-time Day at Main/Mukono campus

Minimum Requirement
In addition to the other University admission requirements for undergraduate Programmes, one of the following categories will allow admission to this course:
- Two principal passes at A' level obtained at the same sitting;
- A two-year diploma in Library and information Science or a related field from a recognized institution;
- A Pass in mature-age examination – such candidates must be Ugandan nationals of at least 25 years and have formal education. Those who are successful, in both the written and oral examination, are considered for admission.

Programme Length
Three years, including at least a one-semester internship, with maximum of five years to finish

Programme Highlights
Information is a key resource for personal, organizational, national and international de-velopment. It must therefore be generated, processed, stored, and disseminated. However, because it is a non-dynamic resource, the above activities cannot happen by themselves. Therefore, there must exist a body of information professionals with extensive theory (knowledge) and training (competence and skills) in order to effectively manage this in-formation based on Christian values and principles.

Courses
Specific course content includes: information science, collection development & manage-ment, communication & technical writing, organization of knowledge, systems analysis & design, database management systems, and management of libraries & information cen-tres, among others.

Career Prospects
Career prospects upon completing this degree can be found in the public and private sec-tor, online media, international organizations, government ministries, departments and agencies. Positions include: archives and records manager, children's librarian, intelli-gence analyst, electronic resource librarian, information officer, Internet trainer, knowledge management specialist, learning resource center librarian and librarian and media specialist.

Faculty of Education and Arts
Department of Education
Bachelor of Science with Education (BSED)
Advent/September Intake – Full-time Day at Main/Mukono campus

Minimum Requirement
In addition to overall university requirements for degree Programme entry, applicants for this Programme must:
- Hold at least the Uganda Advanced Certificate of Education (UACE) or its equivalent with at least two principal passes in subjects related to their choice for major, obtained in the same sitting.

Programme Length
Three years minimum with five years maximum to complete

Programme Highlights
The Bachelor of Science with Education Programme in the Faculty of Education and Arts is designed to enable students explore knowledge in their areas of specialty that could be a combination physics to chemistry, Biology and natural science, mathematics among other combinations as indicated below. Students will develop mastery of their area of specialization and learn to communicate effectively, handle secondary school students with discipline and as role models to promote Christian spiritual and moral formation.

Subject Combinations
- PHY/MATH, BIO/CHEM, MATH/GEO, PHY/CHEM, ECO/MATH, MATH/ICT, BIO/PHY EDUC, BIO/AGRIC, AGRIC/GEO.

Career Prospects
Graduates of this Programme are ready to start a career as professional teachers and education service providers.

Faculty of Education and Arts [educationarts@ucu.ac.ug]

Faculty of Education and Arts
Department of Library and Information Science
Master of Library and Information Science (MLIS)
Advent/September Intake - Modular at Main/Mukono campus

Minimum Requirement
In addition to overall university requirements for degree Programme entry, applicants for this Programme must:
- Hold a second class lower or above under graduate degree from a Chartered University or equivalent interested in offering Programmes in developing a career in Library and Information Studies.

The Department, in consultation with the Dean, School of Research and Graduate Studies, reserves the right to carry out additional assessment to gauge the suitability of candidates for admission.

Programme Length
Two years, with a maximum of four years to complete

Programme Highlights
Information is a key resource for individual, organizational, national and international development. It must therefore be generated, processed, stored, and disseminated. However, because it is a non-dynamic resource, the above activities cannot happen by themselves. Therefore, there must exist a body of information professionals with extensive theory (knowledge) and training (competence and skills) in order to effectively manage this information based on Christian values and principles. The Masters Programme has three main areas of specialization: Information Organization (Library Studies), Records and Archives Management and Information & Communication and trains professionals in all areas.

Courses
Topics within course contents include: information and knowledge management, digitization of Information, management of information systems and services, preservation and conservation of information materials, critical and creative thinking, records & archives management, and knowledge organization, among others.

Career Prospects
Graduates of the Master of Human Resource Management in Education may pursue a teaching or research career related to Library and Information Science.

In brief...

17
The number of programmes in the Faculty of Education and Arts. Of the 17, eight programmes are bachelor's degress, five are master's, two are doctorate and another two are post-graduate diplomas

MLIT
The Master of Arts in Literature is designed to enhance student ability to interpret and analyze cultural, ethical, social and political issues through various types of literature

---

Faculty of Education and Arts
Department of Languages and Literature
Master of Arts in Literature (MLIT)
Easter/January Intake – Modular at Main/Mukono campus

Minimum Requirement
In addition to regular UCU requirements for all students, the following applies:
- First or second-class degree in English/Literature from a recognized university

Programme Length
Two years

Programme Highlights
Through a combination of lectures, discussions and individual research, the Master of Arts in Literature is designed to enhance student ability to interpret and analyze cultural, ethical, social and political issues through various types of literature.

Courses
The eight courses over three modules are on the topics of research, methodology, oral literature, literary criticism, and American, Ugandan, English, Epic and Bible literature.

Career Prospects
Uganda secondary school teachers in the area of English Language and Literature are in demand internationally, including in Rwanda, Burundi and South Sudan. The degree
elevates the graduate's competitive value for academic and research employment especially in relationship to inter-cultural issues, interpretation and analysis with opportunities in teaching, research, creative writing and performing arts.

Faculty of Education and Arts
Department of Languages and Literature
Master of Arts in Translation and Language Development (MATLD)
Easter/January Intake - Modular Main/Mukono campus

Minimum Requirement
In addition to regular UCU requirements for all students, the following applies:
• First or second-class degree in related field of study from a recognized university; and
• Prior knowledge of one indigenous/local language and one foreign/international language.

Programme Length
Two years, with a maximum of five years to complete

Programme Highlights
The Master of Arts in Translation and Language Development Programme is designed for persons interested in intercultural, international communication and exchange, and the development of African languages through personal engagement in translation and free writing.

Courses
Topics within course contents include: translation theories, advanced orthography, editing in African language, history of translation, language policy and translation in multi-lingual societies, research methods, and indigenous/mother tongue and foreign language and terminology development, among others.

Career Prospects
Graduates of this Programme will be qualified to be translators, university lecturers, edi-tors, and writers, among others.

 The Master of Education in Planning and Administration is intended for: current and prospective educational managers/administrators in educational institutions and professional teachers who wish to become lecturers in universities and other tertiary institutions

---

Faculty of Education and Arts
Department of Education
Master of Education in Planning & Administration (MEDAP)
Easter/January Intake - Modular at Main/Mukono campus

Minimum Requirement
In addition to regular UCU requirements for all students, the following are required:
• An honours degree in Education (BED) or (BAED/BSc.ED);
• An honours BA/BSc degree with a Diploma in Education;
• An honours BA/BSc degree with a Post Graduate Diploma in Education (PGDE).

Programme Length
Two years, with a maximum of four years to complete

Programme Highlights
The Master of Education in Planning and Administration aims to prepare students to face the challenging world by producing competent teachers, education managers, lecturers and administrators to carry out various activities that support education and the development of Uganda. This Programme is intended for: current and prospective educational manag-ers/administrators in educational institutions and departments of education at both dis-trict and national levels, professional teachers who wish to become lecturers in universities and other tertiary institutions.

Courses
Topics within course contents include: theories & principles of education administration, student welfare management & administration, academic affairs management & admin-istration, effective teaching & learning in educational Institutions, financial management, and organizational & administration of educational institutions, among others.

Career Prospects
Graduates of the Master of Education in Planning & Administration may pursue a teaching or research career.

Faculty of Education and Arts
Department of Education
Master of Human Resource Management in Education (MHRM)
Easter/January Intake – Modular Main/Mukono campus

Minimum Requirement
In addition to regular UCU requirements for all students, the following requirements apply:
- An honours degree in Education (BED) or (BAED/BSc.ED);
- An honours BA/BSc degree with a Diploma in Education;
- An honours BA/BSc degree with a Post Graduate Diploma in Education (PGDE);
- An honours degree in any other field other than education from a recognized university or institution of higher learning.

The Department, in consultation with the Dean, School of Research and Post-Graduate Studies, reserves the right to carry out additional assessment to gauge the suitability of candidates for admission.

Programme Length
Two years, maximum of four years to complete

Programme Highlights
Organizations including educational institutions exist and operate in a complex political, economic, social and technological environment which is always changing. It, therefore, requires effective management of personnel or employees for an organization to achieve its objectives and successful performance. This Programme trains skill managers who can work well with human persons to best engage organizational strategies in order to work towards the common good.

Courses
Topics within course contents Human Resource Management (HRM): policy in Human Resources, planning, recruitment, screening and selection, job analysis and design, HR training and development, public relations & customer care in educational institutions, employee/industrial relations, and health & safety in educational institution, among others.

Career Prospects
Career prospects upon completing this master's degree can be found in local, national and international government, non-profit and private sectors in the areas of human resource and education, as well as possibly in teaching or research careers.

Faculty of Education and Arts
Department of Languages and Literature
Doctor of Philosophy (PhD), Programme in Literature (PhDL)
Easter/January intake – Modular at Main/Mukono campus

Minimum Requirement
In addition to regular UCU requirements for all students, the following apply:
- Bachelor's degree in Literature, English Language and Literature, or Education with Language/Literature from a recognized university; and
- Master's degree in Literature of English Language and Literature from a recognized university;
- Certified and approved equivalents of the above.

Programme Length
Three years, with a maximum of six years to complete

Programme Highlights
The UCU Department of Languages and Literature, established in 2003, launched a PhD in Literature in 2014. This Programme is designed to broaden and deepen BA and MA Programmes with a higher level of intellectual and analytical engagement with historical, theoretical and regional perspectives.

Courses
Content within this Programme include module and private research dealing with: African, English, European novels, 20th century American poetry, and research design, methods and writing, among others

Career Prospects
Upon completing this degree, students are qualified to expand their careers in writing, editing, publishing and teaching, including at the university level.

Faculty of Education and Arts
Department of Education
Doctor of Education Administration and Management (PEAM)
Easter/January Intake – Modular, Main/Mukono campus

Minimum Requirement
In addition to regular UCU requirements for all students, the following apply:
- Master's degree in education administration and management; OR
- Certified and approved equivalents of the above.

Programme Length
Three years, maximum of six years to complete

Programme Highlights
The doctoral-level study of education administration and management is a fairly new concept on the African continent. The Doctor of Education Administration and Management Programme includes face-to-face discussions with subject-matter experts as well as individualized research that is designed to elevate education administrators to a higher level of quality management for a better business model of solutions and professionalism.

Courses
Content within six courses offered in the first three modules includes: education management models, organization management differences, history of human relations and social science movements, classic and modern administration theories, paradigm of theory and research and Africa empirical evidence in organizational theory.

Career Prospects
Upon completing this degree, students are qualified to better lead education organizations and institutions as well as to teach at the university level.

Three
The number of years a student is required to complete either of the two doctorate programmes in the Faculty of Education and Arts. Failure to complete the doctorate programme within three years, a student is accorded another three years within which to wind up the programme

Faculty of Education and Arts
Post Graduate Diploma in Education (PGDE)
Easter/January and Trinity/May Intakes - Modular at Main/Mukono campus

Minimum Requirement
In addition to overall university requirements, applicants for this Programme must be in possession of a Bachelor's, Master's or PhD from an institution recognized by the National Council for Higher Education.

Programme Length
One year with up to three years to finish

Programme Highlights
The Post Graduate Diploma in Education Programme leads to broad basic qualifications that cover the entire spectrum of professional teacher's foundation. Not only do students acquire specialized know-how, emphasis is also placed on the training of key competencies.

Courses
Specific content includes: history of education, education psychology, curriculum and education technology, education administration and management, philosophy of education, general teaching methods, specific subject teaching methods and comparative education, among others.

Career Prospects
Graduates of this Programme are qualified to teacher in higher education and to write and present research and other writings for conferences and various publications and books.

 **The Post Graduate Diploma in Education Programme leads to broad basic qualifications that cover the entire spectrum of professional teacher's foundation. Not only do students acquire specialized know-how, emphasis is also placed on the training of key competencies**

Faculty of Education and Arts
Post-Graduate Diploma in Higher Education (PGDHE)
Trinity/May and January/Easter intakes, Modular at Main/Mukono campus

Minimum Requirement
In addition to overall university requirements, applicants for this Programme must be in possession of a Bachelor's, Master's or PhD degree from an institution recognized by the Ugandan National Council for Higher Education.

Programme Length
One year

Programme Highlights
This Programme is tailored for individuals who are currently teaching and those who intend to teach in higher educational institutions such as licensed and chartered public and private universities, colleges, Health and training institutions, without any professional training as instructors. The curriculum supports academics that wish to consolidate, develop, and enrich their own practice as part of their professional development.

Courses
Content includes: theory and practice of teaching and learning in higher education, assessment and evaluation in higher education, teaching and classroom management, developing higher education curricular, health and safety management in higher education and communication for teaching and learning, among others.

Career Prospects
This diploma Programme was created to enable current or aspiring leaders interested in developing their leadership ability to advance their higher education skills and knowledge and effectively influence change while supporting growth in student learning. Those who have completed the Graduate Diploma in Higher Education will have demonstrated competency across a variety of essential leadership components.

FACULTY OF JOURNALISM, MEDIA AND COMMUNICATION

ABOUT THIS FACULTY

The Faculty of Journalism, Media and Communication, since its inception in mid 2018, has trained and continues to train a cadre of Journalism, Media and Communication professionals with Christian values.

The faculty offers courses in Mass Communication and Journalism at both Undergraduate (Main Campus) and Postgraduate levels (Kampala Campus) as well as short courses.

The faculty is headed by the Dean, Prof. Monica B. Chibita (B.A/ED, MA, D.LITT. ET PHIL.), along with Heads of Department, Dr. Angella Napakol (Communication) and Dr. Emily Comfort Maractho (Journalism).

FACULTY OF JOURNALISM, MEDIA AND COMMUNICATION

Programme list as of February 2020
1. Bachelor of Arts in Mass Communication (BAMC)
2. Master of Arts in Journalism and Media Studies (MAJMS)
3. Master of Arts in Strategic Communication (MASC)

Mass Communication students prepare to shoot a video interview

PROGRAMMES OVERVIEW

Bachelor of Arts in Mass Communication (BAMC)
Advent/September Intake - Full-time Day at Main/Mukono campus

Minimum Requirement
In addition to the other University admission requirements for undergraduate Programmes, one of the following categories will allow admission to this course:
- Two principal passes at A'level obtained at the same sitting; OR
- A two-year diploma in Journalism, Media Studies, Communication or a related field from a recognized institution;
- A Pass in mature-age examination

Programme Length
Three years, including at least a one-semester internship, with maximum of four years

Programme Highlights
The faculty of Journalism, Media, and Communication focuses on training a cadre of Journalism, Media and Communication professionals with critical literacy in media, diverse professional skills, and with exemplary Christian values. Students study theory, do research and apply concepts in each, and complete resume-building internships. This Programme has two specialization tracks: Journalism and also Communication; the specialization track is selected in the final year of study.

Courses
Specific content includes: media theory, literature in the media, feature writing, contemporary issues, general radio and TV production, broadcast news reporting and current affairs, media ethics, public relations strategy, digital/online communication, radio drama, social and behavior change communication, and investigative journalism and development journalism, among others.

Career Prospects
Career prospects upon completing this degree can be found in the public and private sector in mainstream media, online media, international organizations, government ministries, departments and agencies. Positions include reporter, editor, photographer, communications assistant, public relations officer, and teacher.

Supreme Court Justice Mike Chibita, Prof. Monica Chibita and Vice-Chancellor Dr John Senyonyi at Uganda Christian University, Mukono on January 17, 2020. This was during Prof. Monica Chibita's inaugural professorial lecture, titled Between Freedom and Regulation: Reflections on the Communication Landscape in Uganda

Master of Arts in Journalism and Media Studies (MAJMS)
Advent/September Intake - Modular at Kampala Campus

Minimum Requirement
To qualify for admission to this Programme, beyond all other normal postgraduate Programme requirements, one of the following categories will allow admission to this course:
- Minimum of a Second-Class Bachelor's Degree (or equivalent GPA) in Journalism, Media Studies, Communication or related discipline;

OR
- Minimum of a Second-Class Bachelors' degree (or equivalent GPA) in any field, (with a preference for the Social Sciences and Humanities), plus a minimum of two years' journalistic experience in a recognized media environment;

OR
- Minimum of a Second-Class Bachelors' degree (or equivalent GPA) in any field, plus a postgraduate qualification (equivalent to a diploma) in Journalism, Media Studies, Mass Communication or related discipline;

OR
- Minimum of a Second-Class Bachelors' degree (or equivalent G.P.A) in any field, plus at least two academic or industry publications in Journalism, Media Studies, Communication or related discipline.

Programme Length
Two years (One month of contact study per year in each of February and August)

Programme Highlights
The Faculty of Journalism, Media, and Communication started this Master's course to introduce students to the different facet of Journalism and Media Studies at the postgraduate level. Christian values and ethics are woven throughout the Programme, alongside detailed coursework in journalism and media. The Programme has two specialized tracks for students to select, Research and Professional, with the second having greater emphasis on work applications.

Courses
Among topics covered in courses are: social and gender justice, development, information communication technology, multimedia production, methods of research, editorial management and media policy, law and regulation, among others.

Career Prospects
Career prospects upon completing this master Programme are in the mainstream media, government, international organizations, multimedia, professional production, research and advocacy. Job positions range from reporter, producer, and editor to university lecturer.

Master of Arts in Strategic Communication (MASC)
Advent/September Intake - Modular at Kampala Campus

Minimum Requirement (to be determined by admitting body)
To qualify for admission to this Programme, beyond all other normal postgraduate Pro-gramme requirements, one of the following categories will allow admission to this course:
- Minimum of a Second-Class Bachelor's degree (or equivalent GPA) in Journalism, Media Studies, Communication or related discipline;

OR
- Minimum of a Second-Class Bachelors' degree (or equivalent GPA) in any field, (with a preference for the Social Sciences and Humanities), plus a minimum of two years' journalistic or communication experience in a recognized media environment;

OR
- Minimum of a Second-Class Bachelors' degree (or equivalent GPA) in any field, plus a postgraduate qualification (equivalent to a diploma) in Journalism, Media Studies, Mass Communication or related discipline;

OR
- Minimum of a Second-Class Bachelors' degree (or equivalent GPA) in any field, plus at least two academic or industry publications in Journalism, Media Studies, Com-munication or related discipline.

Programme Length
Two years (One month of contact study per year in each of February and August).

Programme Highlights
A deliberate strategy helps an organization "break through the noise," understand consum-er behavior and master and adapt to an evolving landscape while monitoring and being in-formed by performance metrics. The Masters of Arts in Strategic Communication Pro-gramme, housed within the Faculty of Journalism, Media, and Communication, is designed to elevate journalists and communicators above the rest by not just doing tasks but plan-ning and evaluating projects in the media ecosystem with wisdom, a wide background of knowledge, and a foundation of Christian values.

Courses
Among topics covered in courses are: principles and practices of strategic communication, organisational communication, social and gender justice, development communication, multimedia production, persuasion and advocacy and media policy, law and regulation, among others.

Career Prospects
Career prospects upon completing this master Programme are in public and private sectors and non-profit sector as corporate communicators, consumer communicators, advocacy, and research experts, among others.

TO APPLY...

www.ucu.ac.ug/faculty-of-journalism-media-communication

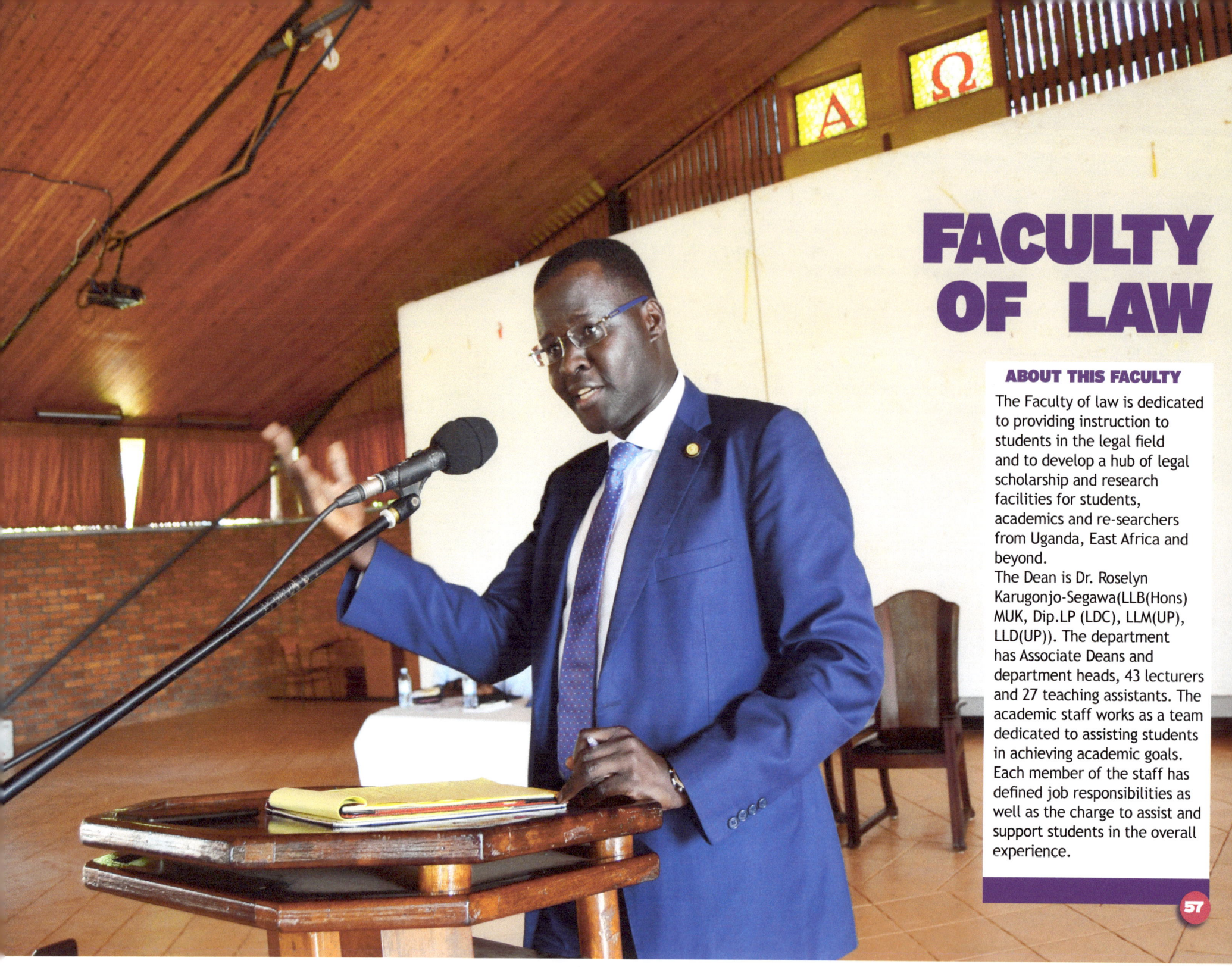

FACULTY OF LAW

ABOUT THIS FACULTY

The Faculty of law is dedicated to providing instruction to students in the legal field and to develop a hub of legal scholarship and research facilities for students, academics and re-searchers from Uganda, East Africa and beyond.

The Dean is Dr. Roselyn Karugonjo-Segawa(LLB(Hons) MUK, Dip.LP (LDC), LLM(UP), LLD(UP)). The department has Associate Deans and department heads, 43 lecturers and 27 teaching assistants. The academic staff works as a team dedicated to assisting students in achieving academic goals. Each member of the staff has defined job responsibilities as well as the charge to assist and support students in the overall experience.

FACULTY OF LAW

Programme list as of February 2020
1. Bachelor of Laws (LLB)
2. Master of Laws in International Business Law (LLM-IBL)
3. Master of Laws in International Energy Law and Policy (LLM-IELP)
4. Master of Laws in Oil and Gas (LLM-OG)

PROGRAMMES OVERVIEW

Faculty of Law
Bachelor of Laws (LLB)
Advent/September Intake - Full-time Day at Mukono/Main campus and Kampala campus; and
Easter/January Intake - Evening at Kampala campus

Minimum Requirement
In addition to the other University admission requirements for undergraduate Programmes, one of the following categories will allow admission to this course:
- Uganda Advanced Certificate of Education with at least 2 principal passes at the same sitting;
- A Diploma in Law from the Law Development Centre or from an accredited university with our without work experience; or
- Undergraduate Degree from an accredited university. Applicants should note that pre-entry interviews are conducted before admission. Non-English speaking applicants may be required to do an English proficiency test before starting the Programme.

Programme Length
Four years with a maximum period of six years to complete

Programme Highlights
Legal education commenced in Uganda in January 1953. The Uganda Law Society, established in 1956, is the body in charge of Legal Education in Uganda. To become a lawyer in Uganda, a person must have a Bachelor of Laws (LLB) undergraduate degree from a recognized university. It takes four (4) years to complete an undergraduate law degree in Uganda. Since 1998, Uganda Christian University's (UCU's) Law Programme has been at the forefront of providing instruction to students in the legal field in Uganda, as well as devel-oping a hub of legal scholarship and research for students, academics, and researchers from Uganda, East Africa, and beyond. UCU's Programme is unique with its infusion of high-level ethics and Christian values.

Courses
Courses have a wide range of topics, including: constitutional, criminal, contract, adminis-trative, land, labour, family, criminal, insurance, human rights, environmental law, tort, equity and trusts, criminology and penology, among others.

Career Prospects
The career prospects available to a graduate of the UCU Law Faculty are in legal practice. Graduation at the Law Development Centre with a Post Graduate Diploma in Legal Practice is required to be a fully practicing lawyer in Uganda. Generally, graduates are engaged in various areas of private legal practice, advocacy, service with the government such, as working with the judiciary, executive and legislature and academia, and teaching, among other things. UCU alumni are working with private law firms, the Ministry of Justice and Constitutional Affairs in Uganda, the Judiciary of Uganda, the Parliament of Uganda, Busi-ness Corporations, Non-Governmental organizations, and with academic institutions.

Faculty of Law
Master of Laws in International Business Law (LLM-IBL)
Easter/January Intake - Modular at Kampala Campus

Minimum Requirement
In addition to the other University admission requirements for undergraduate Programmes, one of the following categories will allow admission to this course:
- (a) Undergraduate degree with minimum second-class lower (2:2) grade;
- (b) Post-graduate Diploma;
- (c) Undergraduate degree with less than second-class grade but at least five years of relevant experience. Additionally, non-English speaking applicants may be required to do an English proficiency test)

Programme Length
12 months for full-time and 24 months for part-time with a maximum of four years to complete. Both full-time and part-time courses include a dissertation.

Programme Highlights
This Master's Programme developed by the Faculty of Law at Uganda Christian University focuses on legal information related to advising, advocating and representing a clients' business interest or issues involving two or more countries. A key goal of the Programme is to prepare lawyers to handle complex issues arising out of international banking, trade and business with legal knowledge, critical thinking, and a strong Christian ethical foundation.

Courses
Examples of courses topics in the Programme are: WTO law and policy, international intellectual property law, EU commercial law and transactions, international trade law, conflict resolution in international business, EU internal market law, and EU intellectual property law.

Career Prospects
There are a variety of Career Prospects for graduates of this postgraduate degree including legal practice in international business-related companies, working as a global investigator, or the work of a corporate law co-ordinator.

LLM-OG — The Master of Laws in Oil and Gas focuses on developing knowledge of the key issues in the emerging oil and gas industry, in addition to increasing a student's analytical and research skills and information analysis

---

Faculty of Law
Master of Laws in Oil and Gas (LLM-OG)
Advent/September, Easter/January, Trinity/May - Modular at Kampala Campus

Minimum Requirement
In addition to the other University admission requirements for undergraduate Programmes, one of the following categories will allow admission to this course:
- (a) Undergraduate degree with minimum second class lower (2:2) grade;
- (b) Pass degree with at least five years experience of relevant experience
- (c) Post-graduate Diploma.

Additionally, non-English speaking applicants may be required to do an English proficiency test.

Programme Length
15 months including research project, with a maximum of four years to complete Programme

Programme Highlights
This Master's Programme developed by the Faculty of Law at UCU focuses on developing knowledge of the key issues in the emerging oil and gas industry. Beyond this, this post-graduate degree also aims to increase analytical and research skills in terms of information analysis relating to legal, economic and environmental problems concerned with the oil and gas industry as well as to allow students to gain exposure to a multidisciplinary learning environment.

Courses
Course topics include: sources of oil, oil and gas regulations, energy law and policy, oil and gas contracting, project financing of natural resource and energy, petroleum resources taxation, environmental aspects of oil and gas and international arbitration, among others.

Career Prospects
Graduates of this Programme will be qualified to practice law in sectors related to issues in the emerging oil and gas industry. These include but are not limited to determining ownership for the right to mine oil and gas, conditions minors have to follow, and regulations governing harvesting of these resources.

Faculty of Law
Master of Laws in International Energy Law and Policy (LLM-IELP)
Easter/January Intake - Modular at Kampala Campus

Minimum Requirement
In addition to the other University admission requirements for undergraduate programmes, one of the following categories will allow admission to this course:
- All applicants need to have an Undergraduate degree (LLB) with a minimum second lower (2:2) grade.
- Non English speaking applicants may be required to do an English proficiency test before being fully enrolled.

Programme Length
This will be a 24-month programme delivered in 4 semesters. A total of 4 modules will be on offer each semester and the last semester will also include the dissertation. A student will need to pass all modules inclusive of the dissertation to obtain this LLM degree.

Programme Highlights
The Master of Laws in International Energy Law and Policy (LLM-IELP) programme is intended to introduce students to Policy issues faced by host countries relating to management of the energy sector. It will also teach students the different legal regulatory and policy considerations by host governments in the management of the energy sector. This course will take students through different types of contracts used in the energy sector and the policy considerations behind them.

Courses
Examples of courses topics in the programme are: International Energy Law and Policy, International Comparative Contractual Law and Policy, Renewable Energy Law and Policy, Renewable Energy Law and Policy, Energy Economics and Finance, International Arbitration, The Oil and Gas Industry and Petroleum and Natural Resources Taxation.

Employment Opportunities
There are a variety of employment opportunities for graduates of this postgraduate degree including international and national energy companies, state electricity and gas companies, government energy ministry, regulatory authorities in energy, policy development, regulation and regulatory compliance, banks and insurance companies, international organisations and non-governmental organizations, law firms; and advisory or consultancy firms.

Law students receive ballot papers for the UCU Law Society's elections

FACULTY OF SCIENCE AND TECHNOLOGY

ABOUT THIS FACULTY

The Faculty of Science and Technology since its inception has trained and continues to train a cadre of technical professionals with Christian values. The faculty offers courses in Computing and Information Technology, Engineering and Environment and Agricultural and Biological Sciences.

The Faculty is headed by Dean, Associate Professor Elizabeth Balyejjusa Kizito (BSc. Agric, PhD). The three departments are headed by the following: Dr. Richard Sembatya (Computing & Technology), Mr. Rodgers Tayebwa (Engineering & Environment) and Ms. Sheila Namuwaya (Agriculture and Biological Sciences).

FACULTY OF SCIENCE AND TECHNOLOGY

Programme list as of February 2020

1. Diploma in Entrepreneurship & Information Technology (DEIT)
2. Bachelor of Agricultural Science and Entrepreneurship (BASE)
3. Bachelor of Aquaculture & Fisheries Management (BAFM)
4. Bachelor of Computational Science (BCS)
5. Bachelor of Electronics & Communication Science (BECS)
6. Bachelor of Environmental Science (BES)
7. Bachelor of Science in Agribusiness (BSAG)
8. Bachelor of Science in Civil and Environmental Engineering (BSCEE)
9. Bachelor of Science in Computer Science (BSCS)
10. Bachelor of Science in Construction Project Management (BSCPM)
11. Bachelor of Science in Food Science and Technology (BFST)
12. Bachelor of Science in Information Technology (BSIT)
13. Postgraduate Diploma in Water and Sanitation (PGDWATSAN)
14. Master of Information Technology (MIT)
15. Master of Science in Agribusiness and Entrepreneurship (MAG)
16. Master of Science in Agriculture and Rural Development (MARD)
17. Master of Science in Environmental Science by Research (MES)
18. Master of Science in Agriculture by Research (MSAR)
19. Master of Science in Water and Sanitation (MSWATSAN)

PROGRAMMES OVERVIEW

Faculty of Science and Technology
Department of Engineering and Environment
Bachelor of Environmental Science (BES)
Advent/September Intake – Full-time Day classes at Main/Mukono campus

Minimum Requirements
In addition to the other University admission requirements for undergraduate Programmes, one of the following categories will allow admission to this course:
- UACE or its equivalent with at least two principal passes at the same sitting, one of which is any of the A level subjects in Biology, Physics, Chemistry, Mathematics, Food and nutrition, Agriculture, Economics, Entrepreneurship, Geography
- Diploma from a recognized institution of higher learning in a relevant field
- A Pass in mature-age examination – such candidates must be Ugandan nationals of at least 25 years and have formal education. Those who are successful, in both the written and oral examination, are considered for admission.

Programme Length
Three years, with maximum of five years to complete

Programme Highlights
This three-year full-time multidisciplinary Programme integrates knowledge and management of complex interactions between natural environmental processes, the environment and human activities, with emphasis placed on sustainable development and environmental management.

The knowledge and skills imparted to BES graduates include widely applicable expertise in information technology, environmental microbiology, environmental chemistry, GIS, environmental economics, environmental policy, law and ethics, EIA, environmental modelling, and other emerging technologies. Graduates also are well-equipped for further education at postgraduate level anywhere in the world.

Career Prospects
The Environment Programmes are aimed at equipping graduates with the knowledge, skills, and scientific basis to develop and/or maintain appropriate and sustainable technical solutions to environmental problems such as: pollution mitigation, climate change adaptation, waste management and remediation. Graduates can work as district environment officers, environmental analysts, Environmental Impact Assessment (EIA) experts, environment Inspectors, lecturers, NGO project managers, environmental consultants, researchers, among others.

Faculty of Science and Technology
Department of Engineering and Environment
Bachelor of Science in Construction Project Management (BSCPM)
Advent/September Intake - Full-time Day at Main/Mukono campus

Minimum Requirements
In addition to the other University admission requirements for undergraduate Programmes, one of the following categories will allow admission to this course:
- Uganda Advanced Certificate of Education (UACE) certificate with at least 2 principal passes (one in either Mathematics or Physics) at the same sitting; and with at least a subsidiary pass in either: Geography, Physics, Chemistry, Biology, economics, Entrepreneurship and/or Mathematics
- Uganda Certificate of Education (UCE) certificate with at least a credit in Mathematics, Chemistry, and Physics
- Diploma from a recognized institution of higher learning in a relevant field
- A Pass in mature-age examination – such candidates must be Ugandan nationals of at least 25 years and have formal education. Those who are successful, in both the written and oral examination, are considered for admission

International applicants
- Applicants must have qualifications that are recognized for University entry in their respective countries for a Bachelor of Science in Construction Project Management or equivalent.

Programme Length
Three years, with maximum of five years to complete

Programme Highlights
This is a 3-year full-time Programme which focuses on understanding infrastructure construction and project management processes.

The interdisciplinary curriculum is based on construction technology and project management principles. At its core is the idea of effectively promoting construction industry development through excellent professional managerial skills.

Career Prospects
The Programme produces professionals who are able to deal with local and global construction project management issues, both academically and practically. The Programme is aimed at equipping graduates with knowledge and skills that will enable them work as construction project managers, independent consultants and researchers as employees of national or international organizations and members of multi- and interdisciplinary teams.

Faculty of Science and Technology

Department of Engineering and Environment
Master of Science in Environmental Science by Research (MSENVSCI)

Advent/September and Easter/January- Full-time Day at the Main/Mukono campus

Minimum Requirements

MSENVSCI is a 2-year Programme and applications can be made year-round for the next in-take. Entry requirements:
(a) holders of at least a Second -Class degree, or equivalent qualification in relevant subject areas
(b) holders of another class of degree in the same disciplines and with a relevant postgraduate diploma or at least two (2) years of field experience and evidence of research publication since graduation
(c) holders of equivalent qualifications from a recognized institution of Higher Education

Programme Length

Two years, with maximum of four years to completion

Programme Highlights

Graduates acquire academic and practical knowledge for promoting integrated science, planning, policy, and education for understanding earth-system processes and managing the impacts of human activity and poverty.

The Programme targets bright students with high interest in research and publication, and is based on the availability of project or personal research funds.

Career Prospects

The Environment Programmes are aimed at equipping graduates with the knowledge, skills, and scientific basis to develop and/or maintain appropriate and sustainable technical solutions to environmental problems such as: pollution mitigation, climate change adaptation, waste management and remediation. Graduates can work as district environment officers, environmental analysts, Environmental Impact Assessment (EIA) Experts, Environment Inspectors, Lecturers, NGO Project Managers, Environmental Consultants, Researchers, among others.

Faculty of Science and Technology

Department of Engineering and Environment
Bachelor of Science in Civil and Environmental Engineering (BSCEE)

Advent/September Intake - Full-Time Day on Main/Mukono campus

Minimum Requirements

In addition to the other University admission requirements for undergraduate Programmes, one of the following categories will allow admission to this course:
• UCE & UACE Certificate with 2 Principal Passes in Physics and Mathematics (MUST);
• Diploma from a recognized institution of higher learning in a relevant field
• A Pass in mature-age examination – such candidates must be Ugandan nationals of at least 25 years and have formal education. Those who are successful, in both the written and oral examination, are considered for admission.

Kenyan Applicants for Degree should hold one of the following:
• KCSE holders must have a minimum grade of C+ and above;
• KACE, 'GCE or A-levels' applicants must have at least 2 principal passes or its equivalent;
• A Diploma in a relevant discipline from a recognized institution of Higher Learning

Tanzanian Applicants for Degree should hold at least either:
• TCE & TACE Certificate with at least 2 Principal Passes;
• Diploma from a recognized institution of Higher Learning.

Other International Applicants
• International applicants must have qualifications that are recognized for University entry in their respective countries

Programme Length

Four years, with maximum of six years to complete

Programme Highlights

The main objective of this 4-year full-time Programme is to educate students to achieve sufficient engineering knowledge, skills and specialization to meet demands of the job market and the national development objectives.

Civil & Environmental Engineers apply science and technology to develop engineered solutions to environmental, public health, and ecological problems. They deal with issues in water supply and sanitation, waste management, pollution control, construction, health and safety, environmental monitoring, planning and management, environmental data collection and analysis, operation and maintenance, etc. Graduates are well-equipped for further education at postgraduate level anywhere in the world.

Career Prospects

The Engineering Programmes train skilled, versatile, professional and ethical graduates for the national and international workplace. This enables them to practice as professional en-gineers upon graduation and meeting requirements for registration by the professional board. Graduates can work as district engineers, consultants; project engineers, lecturers, project managers, researchers, among others.

Faculty of Science and Technology
Department of Engineering and Environment
Master of Science in Water and Sanitation (MSWATSAN)
Trinity/May Intake - Modular at Main/Mukono campus

Minimum Requirements
MSWATSAN is a two-year modular Programme and applications can be made year-round for the next intake. Entry requirements:
(a) a Bachelor's degree in relevant fields
(b) a minimum of two (2) years working experience in a relevant field
(c) fresh University graduates with little or no relevant working experience should have attained a First Class degree or a good Second Class degree to qualify for admission
(d) if necessary, applicants pass an assessment/placement interview conducted by UCU faculty

Programme Length
Two years, with maximum of four years to complete

Programme Highlights
Graduates acquire knowledge and skills to relate the science, technology, and engineering theory to the practice and application in managing water and sanitation services.

The Programme is meant for a small class each year holding various technical, administrative, and managerial positions in public and private water and sanitation utilities, and non-governmental, community-based, and non-profit organizations who work closely with the public in providing water and sanitation in rural and urban areas. The compact modular offering (including an intermediate Postgraduate Diploma in Water & Sanitation) allows practitioners to extend their professional development within their current employment.

Career Prospects
Due to the broad nature of the Programme, a water and sanitation professional usually works as a member of a multi-disciplinary team of specialists team including (bio) chemists, (micro) biologists, epidemiologists, medical workers, environmental scientists, social scientists, social advocates, ecologists, managers, surveyors, and geographers etc. Graduates from this Programme can work in research, academia, industry and non-governmental organizations.

In brief...

2yrs — The number of years of experience an applicant must have to qualify for admission into the Master of Science in Water and Sanitation programme

PGD WATSAN — Students in the Post-Graduate Diploma in Water and Sanitation Programme will gain practical experience through instruction on industry-relevant topics, field work supervision and assessment will be done in partnership with water sanitation utilities and stakeholders

---

Faculty of Science and Technology
Department of Engineering and Environment
Post-Graduate Diploma in Water and Sanitation (PGDWATSAN)
Trinity/May Intake - Modular at Main/Mukono campus

Minimum Requirements
PGDWATSAN is a 1-year modular Programme and applications can be made year-round for the next intake. Entry requirements:
(a) a good Bachelor's degree in relevant fields
(b) fresh University graduates with little or no relevant working experience should have attained a First-Class degree or a good Second-Class degree to qualify for admission
(c) if necessary, applicants pass an assessment/placement interview conducted by UCU faculty

Programme Length
One year

Programme Highlights
In addition to the latest theoretical information provided by subject matter experts, students in the Post-Graduate Diploma in Water and Sanitation Programme in the Faculty of Science and Technology will gain practical experience through instruction on industry-relevant topics, field work supervision and assessment will be done in partnership with water sanitation utilities and stakeholders including the National Water and Sewerage Corporation (NWSC), Directorate of Water Development (DWD) and National Environmental Management Authority (NEMA) among others. This Programme is designed to accommodate a working professional's schedule.

Post-graduate Diploma (PGD): The planned Programme allows flexibility for working professionals in that students successfully completing two (2) taught modules of core and elective course units, and the Fieldwork Assignment and Report, will be able to attain a Post-graduate Diploma (PGD) which can be upgraded by qualified students to an MSc degree up-on completion of an additional year of supervised research, if desired. Credit from the PGD can transfer to an MSc according to guidelines in the UCU Credit Transfer Policy.

Career Prospects
Graduates of this Programme are better prepared to climb the career ladder within or out-side their current employment.

Faculty of Science and Technology
Department of Computing and Technology
Diploma in Entrepreneurship and Information Technology (DEIT)
Easter/January Intake –Full-time Day at Mukono/Main campus

Minimum Requirement
In addition to the other University admission requirements for undergraduate Programmes, one of the following categories will allow admission to this course:
- UCE or its equivalent with a pass in math;
- UACE with at least two point obtained in the same sitting from A' Level;
- A Pass in mature-age examination – such candidates must be Ugandan nationals of at least 25 years and have formal education. Those who are successful, in both the written and oral examination, are considered for admission.

An additional requirement is a Cisco Certified Network Associate (CCNA) certificate obtained not later than six months before entering the Programme.

Programme Length
Two years with four years to finish

Programme Highlights
The Diploma in Entrepreneurship and Information Technology Programme in the Faculty of Science and Technology at Uganda Christian University is specially designed with business and Information and Communications Technology (ICT) components to train students who will be leaders in identifying and pursuing ICT business opportunities to create self sustaining ventures. Students will be equipped for problem solving, innovation, creativity, adaptability and independent learning to keep pace with technology.

Courses
Topics in the content of the coursework includes, among others: information technology, entrepreneurship, information systems, and applications Programmeming, database systems, business economics, Web technologies, computer organization & architecture and principles of management.

Career Prospects
Graduates of this Programme will be employed as computer service/repair technicians, information management officers, ICT research assistants, IT support technicians, ICT project support officers, data officers, among others.

Faculty of Science and Technology
Department of Computing and Technology
Bachelor of Computational Science (Statistics and Financial Maths) (BCS)
Advent/September and Trinity/May Intake - Full-time Day at Main/Mukono campus

Minimum Requirement
In addition to the other University admission requirements for undergraduate Programmes, one of the following categories will allow admission to this course:
- UCE or its equivalent with at least a credit in mathematics and UACE or its equivalent with at least 1 principal passes with the basic sciences;
- A Pass in mature-age examination – such candidates must be Ugandan nationals of at least 25 years and have formal education. Those who are successful, in both the written and oral examination, are considered for admission.

Programme Length
Three years, with maximum of five years to complete

Programme Highlights
The Bachelor of Computational Science Programme aims to produce graduates who integrate mathematical and computing skills in the learning of basic sciences. In addition to the latest theoretical information provided by subject matter experts, students will be introduced to the application of computational science to scientific and industrial problems in a real-world setting and they will have an opportunity to use a range of advanced computing systems such as Matlab, Maple, R and S-plus.

Courses
Topical content in the coursework includes, among others: information technology, principles of Programming, communication technology, computer organization and architecture, discrete maths, probability and statistics, Programming methods, insurance mathematics, mathematical analysis, data analysis and database systems.

Career Prospects
Graduates of this Programme are prepared to start a career in any research environment where computation is the core business. Examples of positions are Programmer analyst, data analyst, information tech manager, research scientist, applied mathematics and risk analyst and bioinformatics specialist.

BCS

The Bachelor of Computational Science Programme aims to produce graduates who integrate mathematical and computing skills in the learning of basic sciences

Faculty of Science and Technology
Department of Computing & Technology
Bachelor of Science in Electronics and Communication Science (BECS)
Advent/September intake - Full-time Day at Main/Mukono campus

Minimum Requirement
In addition to the other University admission requirements for undergraduate Programmes, one of the following categories will allow admission to this course:
- Have UACE or its equivalent with at 2 principal passes in mathematics and physics;
- Possess a diploma of at least second class (lower division) in computing, electronics, telecommunication, or any other diploma that has both mathematics and physics as core components from a recognized tertiary institution.

Programme Length
Four years, with six years to complete

Programme Highlights
The Bachelor of Science in Electronics and Communication Science Programme is designed to focus on the practical aspects and student-centered learning by providing effective integration of practical skills and industry experience well backed by theoretical knowledge in key aspects of engineering. Emphasis is on flexibility to work across many disciplines, preparing students for a variety of professions and identifying the fundamental skills and knowledge that all engineering graduates should posses while providing the understanding engineering-related problems.

Courses
Topics in the course content includes: ICT principles, circuit theory, engineering drawing, structured Programming, information theory and coding, analogue electronics, engineering mechanics, digital electronics, scientific thinking, electronic circuit analysis, mobile communication systems and digital signal processing.

Career Prospects
Graduates of this Programme can be employed as electrical engineers, test/Quality Assurance (QA) engineers, software engineers, computer and information systems managers, IT project managers, service engineers, broadcast and sound technicians, electronic sales managers, electronics and communication consultants and television production managers.

4:6
It takes four years to complete the Bachelor of Science in Electronics and Communication Science, with up to six-year limit for those who stretch beyond the four years. The programme is designed to focus on the practical aspects and student-centered learning by providing effective integration of practical skills and industry experience

Faculty of Science and Technology
Department of Computing and Technology
Bachelor of Science in Information Technology (BSIT)
Advent/September Intake - Full-time Day at Main/Mukono campus; Easter/January Intake - Evening at Kampala campus

Minimum Requirement
In addition to the other University admission requirements for undergraduate Programmes, one of the following categories will allow admission to this course:
- Have a Uganda Certificate of Education (UCE) or its equivalent with at least a credit in mathematics and at least the Uganda Advanced Certificate of Education (UACE) or its equivalent with at least two principle passes in the same sitting;
- Hold a diploma or its equivalent from a recognized institution of higher learning in related courses;
- Engage in the mature-age entry scheme after passing two special mature age University examinations in aptitude and specialized knowledge.

Programme Length
Three years, with five years to completion

Programme Highlights
The Bachelor of Science in Information Technology Programme in the Faculty of Science and Technology aims at preparing students for a professional career in applied computing, E-services and applications. In addition to this, it exposes students to a solid foundation in database systems, Programming practices, networks, E-service and informatics services.

Courses
Topics in the content of the coursework include, among others: information and communication technologies, Web technologies, communication technology, computer organization and architecture, Web applications development, system analysis and design, computer networks, computer graphics, health informatics, database Programmeming and mobile apps development.

Career Prospects
Graduates of this Programme are prepared to start a career in any research environment where information technology is the core business. Example positions within private and non-profit organizations and institutions are systems analysts, information technology managers and officers, network administrators, systems and Web developers, database administrators.

Faculty of Science and Technology
Department of Computing and Technology; Bachelor of Science in Computer Science (BSCS)
Advent/September Intake – Full-time Day at Main/Mukono campus

Minimum Requirement
In addition to the other University admission requirements for undergraduate Programmes, one of the following categories will allow admission to this course:
- At least a credit in mathematics at UCE and passed mathematics plus a good principle pass in any other science or social category subjects at UACE;
- A Diploma or its equivalent from a recognized tertiary institution.

Kenyan Applicants for Degree should hold one of the following:
- KCSE holders must have a minimum grade of C+ and above;
- KACE, 'GCE or A-levels' applicants must have at least 2 principal passes or its equivalent;
- A Diploma in a relevant discipline from a recognized institution of Higher Learning.

Tanzanian Applicants for Degree should hold at least either
- TCE & TACE Certificate with at least 2 Principal Passes;
- Diploma from a recognized institution of Higher Learning.

Other International Applicants
- International applicants must have qualifications that are recognized for University entry in their country.

Programme Length
Three years, with five years to complete

Programme Highlights
The Programme is designed to provide an effective integration of practical skills and industrial experience backed by theoretical knowledge in key aspects of ICT. It consists of two areas of emphasis: systems/network engineering and software engineering/development with a mandatory eight-week industrial placement. The Programme is designed to help students to gain skills in software development and build special interest in object oriented Programming which is relevant to modern application development.

Courses
Topics of the coursework content include: principles of Programming, data structures and algorithms, operating systems, database Programming, computational complexity, web applications development, digital electronics and logic design, information and cyber security, and software construction, among others.

Career Prospects
Graduates of this Programme can be employed as mobile application developers, software engineers, systems architects, machine learning engineers, data engineers, application analysts, CAD technicians, cyber security analysts, database administrators, forensic computer analysts, game designers, IT consultants, machine learning engineers, multimedia Programmers and Web developers.

Faculty of Science and Technology
Department of Computing and Technology; Master of Information Technology (MIT)
Advent/September Intake - Distance Learning with weekend classes of lectures, group discussions and practical assignments

Minimum Requirement
To qualify for admission to this Programme, beyond all other normal graduate Programme requirements, the candidate must hold:
- A Bachelor's degree in Information Systems/Technology, Computer Science, Software Engineering, Computer Engineering or Business Computing with a minimum of a second-class degree (2:2)
- Any other bachelor's degree with evidence of courses in information systems/technology/engineering with a minimum of a second-class degree (2:2).
- ICT-related certification will be an added advantage

Other International Applicants
- International applicants must have qualifications that are recognized for Master's Programme entry requirements in their country equivalent to Ugandan requirements as specified by NCHE.

Programme Length
Minimum of Two years, with maximum of four years to complete

Programme Highlights
The Programme is designed to expand Information Technology theory, methods and support skills as they apply to industry standards and adaptation to current and future trends. Emphasis is on exhibiting professional and ethical behavior when identifying and resolving problems.

Courses
Content coursework includes acquisition and management, strategy and policy planning, enterprise architecture, Programming methods, Internet Programming, data communication and networks, research, project management, security management, modelling, and simulation and financial management.

Career Prospects
Career prospects upon completing this degree can be found in local, national and international government, church, non-profit and private sectors with such titles as: Systems software analyst, web developer, system auditor, web administrator, software developer, network administrator, project management, financial controller, Data analyst and health informatics

Faculty of Science and Technology
Department of Agriculture and Biological Sciences
Bachelor of Science in Agribusiness (BSAB)
Advent/September Intake – Full-time Day Main/Mukono campus

Minimum Requirement
In addition to the other University admission requirements for undergraduate Programmes, one of the following categories will allow admission to this course:
- At least credits in all sciences at the Uganda Certificate of Education examination including two principle passes at the Advanced level in Biology and Mathematics or Economics at the same setting;
- Diploma of at least second-class standing in agriculture, animal husbandry, veterinary or other science-related diploma.

Programme Length
Three years, with maximum of five years to complete

Programme Highlights
The Bachelor of Science in Agribusiness Programme addresses agriculture challenges as mentioned in Uganda's Vision 2040 national development plan regarding constrained socio-economic development. Students are exposed to the most recent advances in information technology and management as applied to improvements in such areas as crop enterprises, qualified staff, climate change, engagement of women and children and funding constraints. Delivery occurs through lectures, personal study, and hands-on activities with real-life case studies.

Courses
In addition to basic foundational skills, topics of coursework content include organic and sustainable agriculture, horticulture, food science, animal production, micro-finance, poultry production, business psychology, climate change and food security.

Career Prospects
Graduates of this Programme will be qualified to provide knowledge and skills for multiple positions designed to help with agriculture systems in East African rural and urban environments.

Faculty of Science and Technology
Department of Agricultural Sciences
Bachelor of Agricultural Science and Entrepreneurship (BASE)
Advent/September Intake – Full-time Day at Main/ Mukono Campus

Minimum Requirement
In addition to the other University admission requirements for undergraduate Programmes, one of the following categories will allow admission to this course:
- UCE or its equivalent with emphasis placed on earning credits in Biology, Chemistry, Mathematics and English along with UACE or its equivalent with at least 2 principal passes in Biology and Chemistry. Agriculture is highly recommended. Economics/ Entrepreneurship, Physics or Geography are relevant;
- National Diploma in the areas of Agriculture, Animal science, crop science and environmental sciences from recognized tertiary institutions;
- A Pass in mature-age examination – such candidates must be Ugandan nationals of at least 25 years and have formal education and a background in agriculture/entrepreneurship. Those who are successful, in both the written and oral examinations, are considered for admission.

Programme Length
Four years including a research project

Programme Highlights
Relevant knowledge of agricultural entrepreneurship is essential to improve livelihoods, food, and nutrition security in Uganda. The Bachelor of Agricultural Science and Entrepreneurship Programme focuses on national agricultural research, production and development under the Ministry of Agriculture, Animal Industry and Fisheries in Uganda. It applies food and agribusiness knowledge and skills in product and service delivery and provides instruction on retrieval and analysis of research findings from the end-user scientific community.

Courses
Among the topics in courses are: agricultural botany, agricultural zoology, biochemistry, sustainable agriculture, agribusiness and entrepreneurship, animal productions systems, breeding and reproduction, organic and sustainable crop production, food chemistry, water resources management and pharmacology.

Career Prospects
Graduates of this Programme can get jobs in such careers as agronomists, agricultural advisors, breeders, bank loan officers and agricultural consultants.

Faculty of Science and Technology
Department of Agricultural and Biological Sciences
Bachelor of Science in Food Science and Technology (BSFST)
Advent/September Intake – Full-Time Day at Main/Mukono campus

Minimum Requirement
In addition to the other University admission requirements for undergraduate Programmes, one of the following categories will allow admission to this course:
- Have a Uganda Certificate of Education (UCE) or its equivalent with at least a credit in mathematics, chemistry and physics; along with at least the Uganda Advanced Certificate of Education (UACE) or its equivalent with at least two principal passes in biology and chemistry at the same sitting;
- Hold a diploma or its equivalent from a recognized institution of higher learning in food science, food technology, veterinary science, forestry or agricultural sciences from recognized tertiary institutions;
- A Pass in mature-age examination – such candidates must be Ugandan nationals of at least 25 years and have formal education and a background in agriculture/entrepreneurship. Those who are successful, in both the written and oral examination, are considered for admission.

Programme Length
Four years, with six years to completion

Programme Highlights
The Bachelor of Science in Food Science and Technology Programme is designed to equip students to relate the knowledge taught in the classroom to the practice of management of food production, processing, distribution and natural resource management in the public or private sector and how to apply them in changing the livelihoods of those in the food supply chain business. Further, the course will provide the student with a comprehensive foundation in business ethics, team building, communication, problem-solving, and leadership skills.

Courses
Topics in the coursework content includes: food microbiology, principles of human nutrition, food chemistry, food engineering, basic electrical technology and mechanics, agribusiness entrepreneurship, food processing and preservation, food quality assurance, agribusiness management, financial accounting and post-harvest technology, among others.

Career Prospects
Graduates of this Programme may find employment as quality assurance associates, quality assurance managers, sensory scientists, quality and food safety specialists, food and beverage managers, food scientists, food technologists, food safety and sanitation supervisors, and food science lecturers in private and public institutions.

Faculty of Science and Technology
Department of Agricultural and Biological Sciences
Master of Science in Agribusiness and Entrepreneurship (MABE)

Advent/September Intake - Weekend on Main/Mukono campus; and Easter/January Intake Evening on Kampala campus

Minimum Requirement
In addition to regular UCU requirements for all students, applicants must meet the following:
- Holders of at least a Bachelor's degree, or its equivalent, from an accredited university in agriculture, rural innovations, education, social sciences, business, environmental science, food science, zoology, botany, biochemistry or any other subject area judged relevant from a recognized tertiary institution with a minimum of a second class degree (2:2).

Programme Length
Two years, with four years to complete

Programme Highlights
The Master of Science in Agribusiness and Entrepreneurship in the Faculty of Science and Technology is a weekend Programme that provides students with the experience to independently utilize agribusiness research principles to understand and solve real world problems. It is designed to provide students with critical thinking, knowledge and technical skills they will need to make agriculture the driver of economic growth and development amidst socio-economic and environmental challenges.

Courses
Topics in the content of the coursework in the Programme include, among others: project planning and management in agriculture, research methods, managerial and business economics, graduate seminars, business law, livestock production for development, agribusiness finance & risk management, cooperative business management, agricultural produce & supply chain management and applied econometrics.

Career Prospects
The potential for employment for graduates from this Programme is with industry, end-user organizations and on projects that would give a real-life context as project planners and developers in various agricultural content areas.

Faculty of Science and Technology
Department of Agricultural Sciences
Master of Science in Agriculture and Rural Development (MARD)

Advent/September Intake and Easter/January Intake- Weekend at Main/Mukono campus

Minimum Requirement
In addition to regular UCU requirements for all students, applicants must meet the following:
- Holders of at least a Bachelor's degree, or equivalent, from an accredited university in agriculture, animal production, rural innovations, and/or food science or any other subject area judged relevant from a recognized tertiary institution with a minimum of a second-class degree (2:2).

Programme Length
Two years with four years to complete

Programme Highlights
Agriculture is the economic backbone of most African countries. In Uganda, 85% of the population is engaged in farming. The Master of Science in Agriculture and Rural Development Programme is designed not just to enable employees to be an extension of an organization, but also to demonstrate to farmers how risk can be minimized to enable increased production and income. A candidate may be exempted from up to one-third of courses based on previous studies from institutions recognized by the Senate of Uganda Christian University. Evidence of justification of exemption must be provided and approved by leadership of the Faculty of Science and Technology.

Courses
Among topics covered within 20 different courses are development and policy design, research methodology, organizational leadership and management, gender and sustainable agricultural development, supply chain management, econometrics, livestock production, and post-harvest strategies.

Career Prospects
The premise of this Programme is that agriculture development is about job creators and not job seekers. The main objective is to produce graduates that can facilitate appropriate infrastructure to enable agriculture to lead rural development and reduce rural poverty. This occurs through teaching, communications, strategic planning, monitoring and evaluating roles in various governments, non-profit, and private entities.

MARD

The Master of Science in Agriculture and Rural Development Programme is designed not just to enable employees to be an extension of an organization, but also to demonstrate to farmers how risk can be minimized to enable increased production and income.

Faculty of Science and Technology
Master of Science in Agriculture by Research (MSAR)
Advent/September and Easter/January - Modular Day at the Main/Mukono campus

Minimum Requirement
In addition to regular UCU requirements for all students, applicants must meet the following:
• Holders of at least a Second-Class Lower (2.2) Honours degree, credit or equivalent qualification in Agriculture, Rural Innovations, Education, Social Sciences, Environ-mental Science, Food Science, zoology, Botany and Biochemistry or in any other subject area judged relevant from a University recognized by Senate.

Programme Length
Two years with four years to complete

Programme Highlights
Master of Science in Agriculture by Research provides advanced training in research for sus-tainable natural resource management, economics, planning, management, gender issues, appropriate technology and rural development. The Programme has a substantial self-study element that provides students with the experience of utilizing independently agricultural research principles to understand and solve a real-world problem.

Courses
With emphasis on practical and entrepreneurial aspects of science and technology, the Pro-gramme has four tracks some of the courses covered under each track are: Crop Sciences (Advanced Agronomy, Advanced Pathology, Applied Entomology), Animal Science (Advanced Animal Nutrition, Animal Production, Advanced Animal Breeding), Economics (Advanced Microeconomics, Advanced Macroeconomics, Econometrics), Soil Science (Land use Management, Advanced Plant Nutrition, Advanced Soil Physics) among others.

Career Prospects
The Programme equips students with a range of transferrable skills and attributes sought by diverse employers. Potential employers include research organizations like the National Agricultural Research Organisation (NARO), Ministry of Agriculture, Animal Industry and Fisheries, Banks and microfinance organisations, CGIAR centres, NGOs and agricultural consultancies.

TO APPLY...
www.ucu.ac.ug/faculty-of-science-and-technology

FACULTY OF SOCIAL SCIENCES

ABOUT THE FACULTY

The Faculty of Social Sciences at Uganda Christian University began in 1997 as part of the Faculty of Education, Arts and Sciences. It has since grown into a fully-fledged faculty with an array of courses at both undergraduate and graduate levels. It is currently one of the largest faculties at Uganda Christian University, with over 4,000 students. The Faculty Dean is Associate Professor, Dr. Mary Ssonko-Nabacwa (BA SS, MA. Women Studies, PhD).

FACULTY OF SOCIAL SCIENCES

Programme list as of February 2020
1. Diploma in Social Work and Social Administration (DSW)
2. Bachelor of Development & Social Entrepreneurship (BDSE)
3. Bachelor of Governance and International Relations (BGIR)
4. Bachelor of Human Rights, Peace and Humanitarian Intervention (BHRP)
5. Bachelor of Organization and Development Management (BODM)
6. Bachelor of Public Administration and Management (BPAM)
7. Bachelor of Social Work and Social Administration (BSWASA)
8. Master of Arts in Counseling Psychology (MACP)
9. Master of Development Monitoring and Evaluation (MDME)
10. Master of Development Studies (MDEV)
11. Master of Public Administration & Management (MPAM)
12. Master of Research and Public Policy (MRPP)
13. Master of Social Work (MSW)
14. Postgraduate Diploma in Development Monitoring and Evaluation (PGDME)
15. Postgraduate Diploma in Public Administration and Management (PGDPA)

PROGRAMMES OVERVIEW

Faculty of Social Sciences
Department of Social Work and Social Administration
Diploma in Social Work and Social Administration (DSW)
Advent/September, Easter/January, Trinity/May - Full-time Evening Main/Mukono and Kampala Campus

Minimum Requirement
In addition to regular UCU requirements for all students, the following applies:
- Hold a UCE & UACE Certificate with 1 Principal Pass and 2 Subsidiaries obtained at the same sitting
- International applicants must have qualifications that are recognized for University entry in their respective countries.

Programme Length
Two years with maximum of four years to complete

Programme Highlights
Social work professionals are recognized as leaders in social change, development, empowerment and liberation. Based in Christian principles, the Diploma of Social Work Programme reinforces not only nurturing and caring for the marginalized population, but also provides curriculum and practical application of social justice and human rights and addresses life challenges, wellbeing and respect for diversity.

Courses
Through lectures, discussion and projects requiring critical thinking, foundational, and content-specific knowledge are delivered in courses. In addition to foundation courses focused are writing and study skills, Old and New Testament, in additional to topic courses in psychology, anthropology, sociology, social work, economics, rural development issues, nonprofit organizations, work with elderly and terminally ill, child and family social work and project planning.

Career Prospects
Graduates are qualified for positions that include probation officer, social welfare officer, medical and clinical social worker, child protection officer, career advisor, charity officer, counselor, social activist and youth and adult guidance workers.

Graduates of the Programme of the Diploma in Social Work and Social Administration are qualified for positions that include probation officer, social welfare officer, medical and clinical social worker, child protection officer, career advisor, charity officer, counsellor, social activist and youth and adult guidance workers

Faculty of Social Sciences
Department of Development Studies
Bachelor of Development and Social Entrepreneurship (BDSE)
Advent/September and Easter/January Intakes - Full-Time Day Main/Mukono campus, as well as Bishop Barham University College, Mbale, Arua campuses

Minimum Requirement
In addition to regular UCU requirements for all students, the following applies:
- Two Principle Passes from A' Level or equivalent.

Programme Length
Three years with maximum of five years to complete

Programme Highlights
Serving those in need is a basic Christian principle. These services in health, sanitation, food safety and more are delivered through non-government, non-profit and for-profit entities. Through lectures, course work and real-life, practical experiences, the Bachelor of Development and Social Entrepreneurship in the Faculty of Social Science strives to prepare students to be part of the planning, implementation and evaluation of solutions for the problems of the world and its people. An integral part of this experience is a partnership with the MICAH, a community, civic and health-based transformation project.

Courses
Specific topical content in the Programme includes writing and study skills, Old and New Testament, Christian ethics, economic and psychology principles, development theory and practice, research methodology, risk management, strategic planning, entrepreneurship and NGO-development and urban development.

Career Prospects
Graduates with this degree are qualified to work with local, regional, national and international public and private organizations, including faith-based, community-based and civil society groups. Positions can involve research, teaching, consulting, policy designing, and evaluating to improve the lives of individuals and communities.

Faculty of Social Sciences
Department of Public Administration and Government
Bachelor of Governance and International Relations (BGIR)
Advent/September Intake – Full time Day Main/Mukono campus nd Mbale Constituent College as well as Evening Kampala campus

Minimum Requirement
In addition to regular UCU requirements for all students, the following is required:
- Direct entrants with two A' Level Principle Passes;
- Ideal students in this Programme are people already engaged in local social science work and who have an open-mind and desire for positive change.

Programme Length
Three years, with a maximum of five years to complete

Programme Highlights
As the world grows politically and economically, facilitating national and international relationships with multiple issues becomes increasingly important. Students in the Bachelor of Governance and International Relations in the Faculty of Social Science will gain an in-depth understanding of international affairs and how they impact people locally, nationally and worldwide. One key aspect of learning in this Programme is gain through professional internships.

Courses
In addition to foundational courses in such areas as Christian ethics, math, writing and science, students will learn about such current issues as terrorism and peace and conflict resolution and roles they might play in them. Through lectures, discussions and projects, topics such as public international law, gender fairness, international security, and disaster management will be explored.

Career Prospects
Graduates of this Programme are prepared for master's level studies as well as jobs in government agencies such as the Office of the President, Legislature, Ministry of Defence, and Ministry of Foreign Affairs; and for missions in diplomacy, peace, human rights, and anti-corruption.

Faculty of Social Sciences
Department of Development Studies
Bachelor of Human Rights, Peace and Humanitarian Interventions (BHRP)
Advent/September intake – Full-time Day Main/Mukono campus

Minimum Requirement
In addition to regular UCU requirements for all students, the following applies:
- Direct Entrants with two Principle Passes from A Level or the equivalent.

Programme Length
Three years, with maximum of five year to complete

Programme Highlights
The Bachelor of Human Rights, Peace and Humanitarian Interventions in the Faculty of Social Science aims to shape students to contribute to the development of peace and human flourishing through knowledge and skills related to the promotion of human rights and the ability to engage skillfully in humanitarian interventions of all kinds. The teaching approach in this Programme is highly interactive with group projects, case studies, and individualized research in person and through e-learning resources. In addition to university teaching staff, think-tank researchers and professors from other universities and guest lecturers working actively within humanitarian groups, the press, government and civil societies provide content.

Courses
Content within the courses assists students with understanding Christian principles, human rights and peace building. In addition to foundation courses, topics include ethics of war and peace, sustainable peace, security and development, and risk and disaster management, among others. African traditions will be explored as they relate to peace building and gender and humanitarian responses to crises.

Career Prospects
Graduates of this Programme are prepared to work with local, national, regional and international organizations as initiators, managers, facilitators and promoters of human rights, peace and intervention in crises and post-conflict environments that interfere with human co-existence and survival.

Faculty of Social Sciences
Department of Development Studies
Bachelor of Organization and Development Management (BODM)
Advent/September Intake – Full-Time Day Main/Mukono campus

Minimum Requirement
In addition to regular UCU requirements for all students, the following applies:
- Direct entrants with two Principle Passes from A Level or the equivalent.

Programme Length
Three years, with maximum of five years to complete

Programme Highlights
Services in health, sanitation, food safety and more are delivered through non-government, non-profit and for-profit entities throughout the world. The Bachelor of Organization and Development Management in the Faculty of Social Science strives to prepare students to be part of the planning, implementation and evaluation of solutions for the problems of the world and its people. This course in particular has a strong focus on planning and management of organizations aiming to serve those in need.

Courses
In addition to foundational courses, course content in this Programme include: Christian ethics, economic and psychology principles, development theory and practice, research methodology, risk management, strategic planning, entrepreneurship and human resource management, among others.

Career Prospects
Graduates with this degree are qualified to work with local, regional, national and international public and private organizations as initiators, managers, and facilitators of development intervention. The tasks include research, consulting, policy design and implementation and evaluation.

Faculty of Social Sciences
Department of Public Administration and Government
Bachelor of Public Administration and Management (BPAM)
Advent/September Intake – Full-Time Day Main/Mukono, Kampala, Mbale Constituent College, and Arua campuses

Minimum Requirement
In addition to the other University admission requirements for undergraduate Programmes, one of the following categories will allow admission to this course:
- Two Principal Passes in relevant courses from A Level;
- Diploma from recognized institution;
- Mature individuals with a pass mark of 50% or more from a National Council for Higher Education-recognized adult education center assessment.

Programme Length
Three years, with maximum of five years to complete

Programme Highlights
With the role of government becoming increasingly complex, it is even more important to have highly qualified public administrators focused on ethics, efficiency and effectiveness. The Bachelor of Public Administration and Management in the Faculty of Social Science emphasizes these traits through skill development and knowledge about branches of government and their effective practices. Content and practical skill is acquired with on-campus and e-learning as well as through 20 weeks of experiential learning.

Courses
In addition to foundational courses, topics in the course units of the Programme include political science, public management and administration, statistics, governance, administrative law and processes, disaster management and democracy and human rights, among others.

Career Prospects
Professionals in public administration are needed to make government function well. Administrators not only support government in various roles of tracking data, forming and communicating policy and advising staff but also serve as watchdogs who identify and provide solutions for eliminating waste and curbing corruption.

Faculty of Social Sciences
Department of Social Work and Social Administration
Bachelor of Social Work and Social Administration (BSW)
Advent/September, Easter/January, Trinity/May Intakes – Full-time Day and Evening Main/Mukono, Evening at Kampala campus, Full-time Day and Weekend at Arua campus, Full-time Day at Bishop Barham University College, and Full-time Day at Mbale Constituent College campuses

Minimum Requirement
In addition to the other University admission requirements for undergraduate Programmes, one of the following categories will allow admission to this course:
Direct Bachelor degree applicants
• Two A Level Principal Passes, with at least one in either economics or entrepreneurship.
Diploma applicants
• One A'level Principal Pass;
• Mature Age Exam;
• All applicants are required to complete a departmental interview.

Programme Length
Three years, with maximum of five years to complete

Programme Highlights
Social work professionals are recognized as leaders in social change, development, empowerment and liberation. Based in Christian principles, the Bachelor of Social Work Programme reinforces not only nurturing and caring for the marginalized population, but also provides curriculum and practical application of social justice and human rights and addresses life challenges, wellbeing and respect for diversity.

Courses
Through lectures, discussion and projects requiring critical thinking, foundational, and content-specific knowledge are delivered in courses. In addition to foundational courses, courses include topics in: psychology, anthropology, sociology, social work, economics, rural development issues, nonprofit organizations, work with elderly and terminally ill, child and family social work and project planning, among others.

Career Prospects
Graduates are qualified for positions that include probation officer, social welfare officer, medical and clinical social worker, child protection officer, career advisor, charity officer, counselor, social activist and youth and adult guidance workers.

BSW
The Bachelor of Social Work Programme reinforces not only nurturing and caring for the marginalized population, but also provides curriculum and practical application of social justice and human rights and addresses life challenges, wellbeing and respect for diversity

Faculty of Social Sciences
Master of Arts in Counselling Psychology (MACP)
Trinity/May Intake - Modular on Main/Mukono campus

Minimum Requirement
In addition to overall university requirements, applicants for this Programme will be screened for maturity, character, stability and academic ability. Applicants must:
• Submit a typed manuscript with personal testimony about religious life and experience, goals, passion for career path and references;
• Have a bachelor's degree with high standing and from an accredited university;
• Complete an interview with the university counseling department faculty.

Programme Length
Two years with five years to complete

Programme Highlights
In addition to the latest theoretical information provided by subject matter experts, students in the Master of Arts in Counseling Psychology will gain practical counseling experience in such settings as churches, prisons, schools, hospitals and various industries. This Programme is designed to accommodate a working professional's schedule.

Courses
Specific topical content in the Programme includes: abnormal psychology, psychosexual issues, child psychology, psychological testing, addictions; and grief, HIV/AIDS, palliative, trauma/crisis, marriage and family counseling, among others.

Career Prospects
Graduates of this Programme will be able to expand in their current positions with added knowledge and skill, including Christian principles, as well as gain new employment as teachers or counselors in private and non-profit organizations and other institutions. The populations served might include children, youth, adults and elderly, among others.

Faculty of Social Sciences
Department of Development Studies
Master of Development Monitoring and Evaluation (MDME)
Easter/January & Advent/ Easter Intake - Modular on Main/Mukono campus

Minimum Requirement
In addition to overall university requirements, applicants for this Programme will be screened for maturity, character, stability and academic ability. Applicants must have:
- A relevant honors bachelor's degree or its equivalent from a recognized university;
- A minimum of one year's work experience is an added advantage;
- At least two referees, one must be academic;
- International applicants must have qualifications that are recognized for University entry in their respective countries.

Programme Length
Two years with four years to complete

Programme Highlights
The Master of Development Monitoring and Evaluation (MDME) Programme at Uganda Christian University is designed to serve development practitioners seeking to widen their knowledge and sharpen their skills in dealing with development monitoring evaluation; and planning and management skills.

Courses
Specific topical content in the Programme includes: Development Theories and Strategies, Development Management, Introduction to Development Monitoring and Evaluation, Qualitative Data Collection and Analysis, Monitoring Evaluation tools and frameworks, Consultancy Management, Grant management and Evaluation, Project Management Information Systems, among others.

Career Prospects
Graduates with this degree are qualified to work with local, regional, national and International public and private organizations, community based civil society groups. Positions can involve monitoring and evaluation specialists, researchers, analysts, Programme co-ordinators, consultants, among others.

 **The Master of Development Monitoring and Evaluation is designed to serve development practitioners seeking to widen their knowledge and sharpen their skills in dealing with development monitoring evaluation; and planning and management skills**

Faculty of Social Sciences
Department of Development Studies
Master of Development Studies (MDEV)
September/Advent Intake - Modular at Main/Mukono campus and Trinity/May Intake - Evening at the Kampala Campus-Mengo

Minimum Requirement
In addition to regular UCU requirements for all students, the following applies:
- Applicants for this Programme must have at least a second-class degree or its equivalent in Development Studies, the humanities or any other fields relevant to human service from an accredited university;
- Candidates should demonstrate a commitment to the goal of human emancipation from all form of deprivation.

Programme Length
Two years, with five years to finish

Programme Highlights
The Master of Development Studies Programme at Uganda Christian University is designed to provide development workers and policy makers with practical skills in handling issues of development and policy with commitment, integrity, and firm Christian values.

Courses
In grooming development practitioners seeking to widen their knowledge and sharpen their skills in dealing with development issues, the following topics are covered: development policy design, analysis and implementation, principles of development economics, human resource managements, and gender based violence, international human rights law, and social entrepreneurship, among others.

Career Prospects
At the end of the Programme, students should be able to conduct scientific research that can contribute to evidence-based policy decisions and strategies for poverty reduction, carry out needs assessment, plan, mobilize resources and implement projects as well as monitor and evaluate their effectiveness, identify the societal injustice prevalent today, and be able to respond to them and develop effective development models that can transform society.

Faculty of Social Sciences

Department of Public Administration and Governance

Master of Public Administration and Management (MPAM)

Advent/September Intake - Modular at Main/Mukono campus, and Trinity/May Intake - Modular at Kampala campus

Minimum Requirement
In addition to the other University admission requirements for undergraduate Programmes, one of the following categories will allow admission to this course:
- Applicants for this Programme have successfully completed an honors bachelor degree from any recognized Institution (University) of higher learning with second class and above or its equivalent from a recognized University;
- Applicants with lower qualifications must satisfy the Senate that they have academic growth by evidence of research and peer reviewed publications.

Programme Length
Two years

Programme Highlights
The Master of Public Administration and Management Programme is looking at skilling/training individuals to a career with the government, public service, corporations, civil society organizations, nongovernmental organizations and private sector organizations. The Programme is designed to accommodate a working professional's schedule. Students can select either a dissertation or extra module with a research project in the final year.

Courses
With options for either private or public sector management pathways in year two and requirement of qualitative and quantitative methodology for all, some topical content in this Programme is: Public-private partnerships, Management Information Systems, public management ethics, administrative law and processes, public policy formulation and management, marketing, public relations and management of human resources, procurement and leadership of non-profit organizations, among others.

Career Prospects
The Masters of Public Administration and Management prepares highly professional administrators and managers for the public and private sectors, civil society and nonprofit sectors; and other inter-state organizations. Graduates can pursue careers with a wide scope of employers including public service sector, local governments, central government ministries, security forces, public corporations, and intergovernmental bodies at regional and international levels, private sector investments, civil society organizations of NGOs, and many more.

Social Sciences students from the Department of Public Administration and Governance clean the veranda of a ward at the Mukono Health Centre IV during an outreach

Faculty of Social Sciences
Department of Public Administration and Governance
Master of Research and Public Policy (MRPP)
Trinity/May Intake - Full-time at Mukono/Main campus and Weekend at Kampala campus

Minimum Requirement
In addition to the other University admission requirements for undergraduate Programmes, one of the following categories will allow admission to this course:
- An Upper Second class Bachelor's degree, or higher;
- A Bachelor's degree of a lower second class, and at least 2 years of working experience in a research or policy, or a postgraduate diploma;
- A Masters degree

Programme Length
Two years, with five years to complete

Programme Highlights
The Master of Research and Public Policy housed in the Faculty of Social Science aims to build professional researchers and policy analysts and makers with strong critical thinking skills, deep integrity, and a firm Christian ethical foundation. This Programme is based on priorities of the African Public Policy Agenda and has two specialization tracks: Research or Policy Practice.

Courses
Specific content includes: governance and politics of public policy, social science foundations for public policy, economics for public policy, political economy of public policy, global context of public policy, research methods, and contemporary issues in public policy, among others.

Career Prospects
Career prospects upon completing this Programme can be found in universities, government, research organizations, think tanks, civil society organizations, media, regional and international levels, and private sector investments.

MRPP

The Master of Research and Public Policy aims to build professional researchers and policy analysts and makers with strong critical thinking skills, deep integrity, and a firm Christian ethical foundation

Faculty of Social Sciences
Department of Social Work and Social Administration
Master of Social Work (MSW)
Advent/September Intake - Full-time Main/Mukono, Kampala, and Bishop Barham University campuses

Minimum Requirement
Applicants for this Programme need:
- At least a bachelor degree from an accredited university with a specialty in one of these areas: social work and social administration, sociology, psychology, counseling, health (nursing, physician, etc.), education, nutrition, domestic science, religious and ministerial studies, environment, economics, political science, development studies, management-related course;
- Two years of work experience with computer and English competency;
- Prior research experience;
- Physical fitness for field work;
- and must complete a Faculty interview.

Programme Length
Two-years, with maximum of four years to complete

Programme Highlights
The Master of Social Work Programme in the Social Science Faculty will provide knowledge and skills related to resolution of issues such as relational tensions, domestic violence, mental challenges, child abuse and neglect, gender inequality and socio-economic stresses. Multi-disciplinary approaches are emphasized in lectures, individualized study, and hands-on experiences. The Programme includes fieldwork experience with comprehensive written report and research dissertation

Courses
Topic content in the courses for this Programme includes mental health, social gerontology, substance abuse, health care systems (rural, urban and international), gender development, social welfare and policy analysis, legal systems and social work practice, research, among others.

Career Prospects
At the end of the Programme, graduates will work in health centers, civil society organizations and others as policy makers, researchers, social welfare workers, policy analysts and administrators and advocates for human rights and social justice.

Faculty of Social Sciences
Department of Development Studies
Post graduate Diploma in Development Monitoring and Evaluation (PGDME)
Easter/January & Advent/September Intake - Modular on Main/Mukono campus

Minimum Requirement
In addition to overall university requirements, applicants for this Programme will be screened for maturity, character, stability and academic ability. Applicants must:
- A relevant honors bachelor's degree or its equivalent from a recognized university;
- A minimum of one year's work experience is an added advantage;
- At least two referees, one must be academic;
- International applicants must have qualifications that are recognized for University entry in their respective countries.

Programme Length
One year with three modules and two years to complete

Programme Highlights
The post-graduate Diploma in Development Monitoring and Evaluation (PGDME) Programme at Uganda Christian University is designed to serve development practitioners seeking to widen their knowledge and sharpen their skills in dealing with development monitoring evaluation; and planning and management skills.

Courses
Specific topical content in the Programme includes: Development Theories and Strategies, Development Management, Introduction to Development Monitoring and Evaluation, Qualitative Data Collection and Analysis, Monitoring Evaluation tools and frameworks, Consultancy Management, Project Management Information Systems, among others.

Career Prospects
Graduates with this degree are qualified to work with local, regional, national and International public and private organizations, community based civil society groups. Positions can involve M&E Specialists, researchers, analysts, Programme coordinators, consultants, among others.

Faculty of Social Sciences
Department of Public Administration and Governance
Post-Graduate Diploma of Public Administration and Management (PGDPA)
Trinity/May intake at Kampala campus

Minimum Requirement
Applicants for this Programme must have:
- Bachelor's degree in any discipline from a recognized institution;
- At least two years work experience with some management or, however, those without such experience, should have a First-Class Degree or Second-Class Upper Degree.

Programme Length
One year, with three modules of four weeks each

Programme Highlights
The Post-Graduate Diploma of Public Administration and Management Programme focuses on preparing workers from the smallest local office to the highest halls of executive and legislative power with the ultimate goal of making government and private sector as efficient and effective as possible. In the third module, students choose either Public Management or Private Sector Management pathways and research projects.

Courses
Course content includes: public management in contemporary society, management information system, ethics in public administration, public policy formulation and management, public private partnership, procurement management, research methods, marketing and public relations, among others.

Career Prospects
Career prospects upon completing this Programme can be found in public service, local governments, central government ministries, military systems or security bodies, public corporation, intergovernmental bodies at regional and international levels, private sector investments, CSOs and NGOs. Additionally, graduates can qualify for the UCU Master of Public Administration and Management Programme, providing that application occurs within one year of graduation.

PGDA

The Post-Graduate Diploma of Public Administration and Management Programme focuses on preparing workers from the smallest local office to the highest halls of executive and legislative power with the ultimate goal of making government and private sector as efficient and effective as possible

UCU SCHOOL OF MEDICINE

ABOUT THE FACULTY

The UCU School of Medicine provides career pathways to the medical profession through training medical professionals with Christian values. The school offers Programmes in the following disciplines: Medicine, Dentistry, Nursing, Public Health, and Health Administration.

The school is headed by the Dean, Dr. Edward Kanyesigye (MB.Ch.B, DPH, MPH, with Department leadership as follows: Public Health, Dr. Ekiria Kikule; Nursing, Elizabeth Situma; Maternal and Child Health, Dr. Miriam Mutaabazi; and Health Administration, Dr. Edward Mukooza.

FACULTY OF SCIENCE AND TECHNOLOGY

Programme list as of February 2020
1. Diploma in Health Administration (DHA)
2. Diploma in Nursing (DNS)
3. Bachelor of Dental Surgery (BDS)
4. Bachelor of Environmental Health Science (BEHS)
5. Bachelor of Health Administration (BHA)
6. Bachelor of Medicine & Bachelor of Surgery (MBChB)
7. Bachelor of Nursing Science (BNS)
8. Bachelor of Public Health (BPH)
9. Bachelor of Science in Human Nutrition & Dietetics (BHND)
10. Master of Nursing Science (MNS)
11. Master of Public Health (MPH)
12. Master of Public Health Leadership-Save the Mothers (MPHL)
13. Master of Science in Human Nutrition (MSHN)

PROGRAMMES OVERVIEW

UCU School of Medicine
Department of Public Health
Diploma in Health Administration
Advent/September, Trinity/May – Modular at Main/Mukono campus

Minimum Requirement
In addition to overall university requirements, applicants for this Programme should be:
- Working in a health care system with a minimum of a certificate from a recognized tertiary institution recognized by the National Council for Higher Education.

Programme Length
Two years minimum and four years maximum in a Programme

Programme Highlights
This Programme has been in existence since 1993. It is located under UCU School of Medicine in the department of Public Health. The chief target of the Programme is health workers or anyone in the health care system seeking to build skills in management.

Courses
Topics in the content of the coursework include: human resource management, research methods, organizational behavior, financial account management, counseling, marketing and project planning, among others.

Career Prospects
Graduates of this Programme should have access to higher-level positions of management.

In brief...

3yrs

It takes three years, with a maximum of five years, to complete the Diploma in Nursing Programme. Nurses with a nursing diploma are employed in various health care settings, including, but not exclusively hospitals, health centres, schools, and NGOs.

DHA

The chief target of the Diploma in Health Administration Programme are the health workers or anyone in the health care system seeking to build skills in management

---

UCU School of Medicine
Faculty of Health Sciences
Diploma in Nursing Programme (DNS)
Full-time Day at affiliated Church of Uganda Schools of Nursing, at Kagando School of Nursing and Midwifery, and Bwindi School of Nursing and Midwifery

Minimum Requirement
In order to be eligible for admission to the Programme, beyond the normal UCU admission requirements, a candidate should fulfill all UCU admission requirements for the Diploma Programmes. In addition, eligible candidates:
- Should possess at least an O' level certificate or equivalent qualification obtained at one sitting and at least 1 A' level principal pass in Biology; other science subjects like Chemistry, Health Science, or Nutrition are an added advantage;
- Should be enrolled nurses, i.e. (EN, ECN, E Mid, E. Mental Nurse) after a working experience of not less than 2 years in a recognized health institution;
- Pass an admission interview.

Programme Length
Three years, with maximum of five years to complete

Programme Highlights
The diploma nurse has been identified by the larger health sector in Uganda as the frontline health worker to deliver services to the Uganda population. The Diploma in Nursing Programme at the School of Medicine at Uganda Christian University meets this gap by building a professional cadre of nurses and midwives, with high moral and professional standards, that focus on promoting holistic health care of the clients and the community by strengthening the quality, compassion, and responsiveness of Uganda and East African health care systems.

Courses
This Programme includes study in the following areas, among others: foundations of nursing, human anatomy, microbiology, pharmacology, midwifery, community health, mental health, and general nursing administration and management.

Career Prospects
Nurses with a nursing diploma are employed in various health care settings, including, but not exclusively hospitals, health centres, schools, and NGOs. They are eligible for the Bachelor of Nursing completion Programme (BNS-CP) at UCU.

UCU School of Medicine
Bachelor of Dental Surgery (BDS)
Advent/September Intake - Full-time Day at UCU-Mengo campus

Minimum Requirement
Admission to the Programme requires a prequalification based the criteria listed below, beyond normal UCU requirements, as well as a pre-entry examination. One of the follow categories will allow admission to this course:
- Direct entrants with the Uganda Certificate of Education (UCE) or its equivalent with at least 5 passes, including Math and English, and least 2 A' level principal passes in Biology and Chemistry taken at the same sitting and at least a subsidiary pass in either Physics or Mathematics of the Uganda Advanced Certificate of Education (UACE);
- A credit or class II diploma in a health related discipline with at least a Credit in Biology, Chemistry, Physics, or Mathematics, as well as at least 2 years in a relevant health or dental related field since qualification;
- Admissions by the mature-age entry Examination Certificate issued by a recognized institution or related University Examinations, alongside all other requirements;
- Bachelor's degree in a relevant health subject from a recognized University with a CGPA of at least 4.0.

Programme Length
Five years, with maximum of seven years to complete

Programme Highlights
According to the Uganda Health System Assessment Report in 2011, the dentist to population ratio in Uganda is 1:168,000 compared to the WHO's recommend ratio of 1:1,000. The Bachelor of Dental Surgery Programme in the School of Medicine at Uganda Christian University aims to help close that gap with focus on training dental health professionals who will be leaders and scientists and providing outstanding and compassionate dental health care. The students can select one of several dental disciplines (operative dentistry, endodontics, orthodontics, etc.) as part of their study.

Courses
Topical content in the coursework in the Programme include, among others: physiology, Pathology, Microbiology, medical sociology, biochemistry, pharmacology, oral biology, and restorative dentistry, oral medicine, orthodontics, oral surgery.

Career Prospects
Career prospects upon completing this degree can be found in local, national and international government, non-profit and private sectors with specialties and subspecialties, including orthodontics and dental orthopedics, pediatric dentistry, periodontics, prosthodontics, oral and maxillofacial surgery, oral and maxillofacial pathology, endodontics, public health dentistry, and oral and maxillofacial radiology. They also are eligible to undertake a Masters Degree to further increase their specialty.

UCU School of Medicine
Department of Public Health
Bachelor of Environmental Health Science (BEHS)
Advent/September - Full-time Day at UCU – Mengo Campus

Minimum Requirement
In addition to the other University admission requirements for undergraduate Programmes, one of the following categories will allow admission to this course:
- Holder of a UACE or its equivalent with a minimum of 2 A' level passes with one in biology and the other in any of the subjects of chemistry, physics, agriculture, geography, mathematics, economics, health science;
- Holder of Diploma in Environmental Health Science or any other health-related diploma with a recognized institution;
- A Pass in mature-age examination – such candidates must be Ugandan nationals of at least 25 years and have formal education. Those who are successful, in both the written and oral examination, are considered for admission.

Programme Length
Three years, with maximum of five years to complete

Programme Highlights
With 17% of the world's population having no access to safe water and adequate sanitation, alongside agriculture pesticide challenges, and the evolution of the oil industry, environment health problems are a growing concern. The Bachelor of Environmental Health Science Programme in the School of Medicine at Uganda Christian University strives to address these issues to avoid malnutrition, construction accidents and pollution.

Courses
Addressing the United Nations Millennial Goal 7 on Environmental Stability, courses include topics related to, among others: microbiology, epidemiology, public health nutrition, waste water management, vermin control, biostatistics and natural and alternative medicine.

Career Prospects
Graduates of this Programme will be able to work with other organizations or on their own in various jobs designed to meet community and environmental health fields such as environmental scientist, occupational safety and health officer, environmental health and safety technician, or environmental health consultant.

UCU School of Medicine
Department of Public Health; Bachelor of Health Administration
Advent/September, Trinity/May - Modular at Main/Mukono campus

Minimum Requirement
In addition to overall university requirements, applicants for this Programme should:
- Anyone working in a health care system with a minimum of a Diploma from a recognized tertiary institution recognized by NCHE.

Programme Length
Three years minimum and five years maximum

Programme Highlights
Since 1993, this Programme has been training students to skillfully engage in administering health related Programmes. The Programme targets health workers or anyone in the health care system seeking to grow their skills in managing centres/hospitals/Programmes devoted to human health.

Courses
Topics in the content of the coursework include, among others: human resource management, management theory, organizational behavior, health and the law, health economics, organizational development, social psychology, counseling and organizational sociology.

Career Prospects
Graduates of this Programme usually get promoted into higher-level positions of management as part of a health care system, including in hospitals, health centres, and other health related projects.

UCU School of Medicine
Department of Nursing; Bachelor of Nursing Science
Diploma Completion Programme (BNS-DCP) and Direct Entry (BNS-DE)
I: Easter/January Intake - Full-time Day BNS-DCP at UCU-Mukono/Main campus;
II: Advent/September Intake - Full-time Day BNS-DE at UCU-Mukono/Main campus.

Minimum Requirement
- In order to be eligible for admission to the BNS-DCP Programme, beyond the other admission requirements, one of the following categories will allow admission to this course:
- Possess at least an Ordinary Level (O' level) certificate or equivalent qualification obtained at one sitting and an Advanced level (A' level) certificate or the equivalent qualification obtained at one sitting with a Principal Pass in Biology and Chemistry;
- Have a diploma in General nursing and Midwifery or Comprehensive nursing, registered with Uganda Nurses and Midwives Council with a valid practicing license and a working experience of not less than 2 years in a recognized health facility;
- Additionally, all candidates must pass a Nursing Admission Interview conducted by the University.

II: To be eligible for admission to the BNS-DE, beyond the other admission requirements, one of the following categories will allow admission to this course:
- Possess at least an Ordinary Level (O' level) certificate or equivalent qualification obtained at one sitting and an Advanced level (A' level) certificate or the equivalent qualification obtained at one sitting with two Principle Passes in science subjects both Biology and Chemistry; or
- Diploma entry to the 4-year BNS Programme will be considered for nurses or midwives qualified from a recognized school of nursing and or midwifery or an equivalent health professional diploma. Diploma candidates should possess a valid practicing license and have a working experience of not less than 2 years in a recognized health facility.

Programme Length
I. The duration of the BNS-DCP is 3 years, with maximum of five years to completion
II. The duration of the BNS-DE is 4 years, with maximum of six years to completion

Programme Highlights
The Bachelor of Nursing Science Programme focuses on promoting holistic health care of the clients and the community by strengthening the quality, compassion, and responsiveness of Uganda and East African health care systems through emphasis on building a professional cadre of nurses and midwives with high moral and professional standards.

Courses
Topical content in the coursework of Programme include: foundations of nursing, health assessment, human anatomy and physiology, pathophysiology, microbiology, pharmacology, biochemistry, biostatistics, child health/paediatric nursing, medical and surgical nursing, mental health nursing, midwifery, clinical nursing skills, nursing informatics, nutrition and cultural diversity in health care.

Career Prospects
Nurses with a bachelor's degree in nursing are employed in various health care settings including hospitals, schools, NGOs and health centres. They fit into the career ladder of nurses in the country and are eligible to undertake a Master's Degree in any relevant field to become specialists.

UCU School of Medicine
Bachelor of Medicine and Bachelor of Surgery (MBChB)
Advent/September Intake – Full-time Day at UCU-Mengo campus

Minimum Requirement
Admission to the Programme requires a prequalification based the criteria listed below as well as a pre-entry examination. In addition to these requirements, one of the following categories will allow admission to this course:

- Direct entrants with the Uganda Certificate of Education (UCE) or its equivalent with at least 5 passes, including Math and English, and least 2 A' level principal passes in Biology and Chemistry taken at the same sitting and at least a subsidiary pass in either Physics or mathematics of the Uganda Advanced Certificate of Education (UACE);
- A credit or class II diploma in a health related discipline with at least a Credit in Biology, Chemistry, Physics, or Mathematics, as well as at least 2 years in a relevant health related field since qualification;
- Admissions by the mature age entry Examination Certificate issued by a recognized institution or related University Examinations, alongside all other requirements;

For those who already hold a degree, in order to gain admission to this course, have a bachelor's degree in a relevant science subject from a recognized University with a CGPA of at least 3.5.

Programme Length
Five years, with maximum of seven years to complete

Programme Highlights
The Bachelor of Medicine and Bachelor of Surgery Programme in the School of Medicine at Uganda Christian University aims to advance the local, regional, and global need for ethical, high qualified, diverse medical professionals, leaders, and scientists in order to provide Competent, conscientious, compassionate, and collaborative medical care, pursue new knowledge and excellence of practice, and advocating for the health of all nations.

Courses
Beyond foundational courses, this Programme includes study in the following topics: Anatomy, Physiology, Biochemistry, Behavioural Sciences, Microbiology, Pathology, Pharmacology, Medicine, Surgery, Public Health, Paediatrics, Obstetrics and Gynaecology, Psychiatry, Radiology, Anaesthesia and Ophthalmology.

Career Prospects
Career prospects upon completing this degree can be found in local, national and international government, non-profit and private sectors with specialties and subspecialties, including urology, surgery, radiation oncology, psychiatry, preventive medicine, physical medicine and rehabilitation, pediatrics, Pathology, Ophthalmology, Obstetrics and Gynaecology, Nuclear medicine, Neurology, Medical genetics, Internal medicine, Family Medicine, Emergency medicine, Diagnostic radiology, Dermatology, Anesthesiology, Allergy and immunology.

MBChB

The Bachelor of Medicine and Bachelor of Surgery Programme in the School of Medicine at Uganda Christian University aims to advance the local, regional, and global need for ethical, high qualified, diverse medical professionals, leaders, and scientists in order to provide Competent, conscientious, compassionate, and collaborative medical care

UCU School of Medicine
Department of Public Health
Bachelor of Public Health (BPH)
Advent/September Intake - Full-time Day at Main/Mukono Campus

Minimum Requirement
In addition to normal UCU admission requirements, one of the follow categories will allow admission to this course:
- Direct entrants with the Uganda Advanced Certificate of Education (UACE)
- Two Principal passes at the same sitting in any of the following science subjects; Biology, Chemistry, Agriculture, Food and Nutrition, Geography and Physics
- Diploma entrants with a diploma obtained at credit/distinction level in a professional health science from a recognized university;
- Mature-age Entrants who are aged 25 and above and have passed a mature age entry Examination Certificate issued by a recognized institution or related University Examinations.

Programme Length
Three years, with maximum of five years to completion

Programme Highlights
The Programme aims to train health professionals specifically in the areas of disease control and health promotion.

Courses
This Programme includes study in the following areas, among others: epidemiology, biostatistics, health services management, prevention and control of communicable and non communicable disease, environmental health, reproductive health, among others.

Career Prospects
Upon completing this degree, career prospects can be found in ministries, lead agencies, NGOs, business enterprises, government, schools and other organizations with such titles as: community nutritionist, clinical dieticians, researchers, trainers, health educators, managers, planners, policy makers and food service delivery workers.

UCU School of Medicine
Department of Public Health
Bachelor of Science in Human Nutrition and Clinical Dietetics (BHND)
Advent/September Intake, Full-time Day and (Modular) affiliated to Mildmay Institute of Health Sciences of Mild May Centre

Minimum Requirement
In addition to normal UCU admission requirements, one of the follow categories will allow admission to this course:
- Direct entrants with the Uganda Advanced Certificate of Education (UACE)
- Two Principle passes obtained at the same sitting one of which must be Biology, and the other can be any of the following science subjects; Mathematics, Chemistry, Agriculture, Food and Nutrition, Home Economics and Physics
- Diploma entrants with a diploma obtained at credit/distinction level in a professional health related from a recognized university;
- A Bachelor's degree in any clinical related discipline or in Biology/Sciences
- Mature-age Entrants who are aged 25 and above and have passed a mature age entry Examination Certificate issued by a recognized institution or related University Examinations.

Programme Length
Four years for Direct Entrants and three years for entrants with a Diploma in Human Nutrition

Programme Highlights
The Programme aims to train health professionals specifically in the areas of human diet, food related diseases and management, both community and hospital nutritional management. These professionals are trained in wisely and skillfully implementing nutritional related Programmes.

Courses
This Programme includes study in the following areas, among others: nutrition, human biology, management of nutritional challenges, household food safety & security, among others.

Career Prospects
Upon completing this degree, career prospects can be found in ministries, lead agencies, Referral Hospitals Regional, General and District Hospitals and any organization like church and NGO's that are implementing nutritional related Programmes.

UCU School of Medicine
Department of Nursing
Masters of Nursing Science – Focusing on Nursing Education (MNS)
Trinity/May Intake - Modular and Online between modules at UCU-Mukono/Main campus and Kampala campus

Minimum Requirement
In order to be eligible for admission, candidates need all of the following:
- UCU entry exam passage;
- Must be a Registered Nurse (RN) with current licensure in Uganda;
- Successfully completed a Bachelor's Degree in Nursing (BNS or BSN preferred);
- Demonstrated experience as a nurse educator and/or instructor of nurses or nurse aides;
- Leadership and academic abilities (potentials) and skills (proficiencies);
- Capabilities and demonstrated comfort with computer technology to use on-line tutorials;
- Minimum two years of working experience in a recognized health institution.

Programme Length
The duration of the Programme is 2 years and 4 months, or 28 months total.

Programme Highlights
The Masters of Nursing Science – Focusing on Nursing Education Programme in the School of Medicine focuses on promoting holistic health care of the clients and the community by strengthening the quality, compassion, and responsiveness of Uganda and East African health care systems through emphasis on building a professional cadre of nurses and midwives with high moral and professional standards.

Courses
Content in the following areas are included in the modules of the Programme, among others: pathophysiology, statistics, advanced physical and health assessment, curriculum development in nursing, clinical nursing studies, and nursing informatics.

Career Prospects
Upon completing this degree, the graduates will manage nursing educational Programmes and provide needed leadership as lecturers, department heads, commissioners of health services, etc. at all levels of the nursing profession in various health care setting including schools of nursing, universities, hospitals, health centres, schools, and other local, national, regional, and international organizations. They are eligible to undertake doctoral education to further advance the profession of nurses.

UCU School of Medicine
Department of Public Health
Master of Public Health (MPH)
Easter / February Intake – Modular Programme at Kampala campus

Minimum Requirement
One of the follow categories will allow admission to this Programme:
- Bachelor's degree with at least a Second Class lower division from a recognized university in health disciplines;
- Graduates of Mathematics, Statics and Computer Sciences and Social Sciences with evidence of being employed in the social sector i.e. Professionals; Lawyers, engineers

Programme Length
Two years with three modules per year

Programme Highlights
The Master of Public Health Programme in the School of Medicine at aims to help form more professional public health workers to counter the health challenges in the East African region. The health managers will be responsible for the administration, research, policy formulation, analysis in areas that involve health promotion, disease prevention and health sector management among others.

Courses
In order to establish a cadre of health workers, this course includes the following subjects, among others: public health fundamentals, applied epidemiology and biostatistics, public and community health practice, bioethics and research methods, health economics and health financing, Health Policies, reproductive health, bio ethics and environmental health.

Career Prospects
Upon completing this Masters degree, career prospects can be found in local, national and international government, non-profit and private sectors with such titles as: District health officer, community health worker, health consultant, lecturer, health planner, health advocate, health researcher.

MPH The Master of Public Health Programme aims to help form more professional public health workers to counter the health challenges in East Africa. The health managers will be responsible for the administration, research, policy formulation and analysis

UCU School of Medicine
Master of Science in Human Nutrition (MSHN)
Advent/September Intake - Distance Learning/E-Learning and Modular at UCU-Kampala campus

Minimum Requirement
In order to be eligible for admission, candidates need the following:
- Holders of at least a bachelor's degree, or equivalent, from a recognized tertiary institution with a minimum of a second class degree (2:2).

Programme Length
Two years, with maximum of four years to completion

Programme Highlights
This Master of Science in Human Nutrition Programme in the School of Medicine focuses on forming professionals, including current health, and other related fields, practitioners, to be health specialists in the area of food and nutritional health and so to reduce the impacts of poor nutrition in communities and among persons. Two major emphases are available in the Programme: 1) Community Nutrition and 2) Nutrition and Dietetics. Distance and/or module delivery allows working professionals to obtain a master's degree. Students participate in a 10-week clinical dietetics or community nutrition project work/practicum at the end of their first year, as well as field visit relevant to the course of study.

Courses
Content aimed in the following areas are included in the modules of the Programme, among others: fundamentals of nutrition, health ethics, research design, clinical dietetics, health determinants, biostatistics, public health systems and policy, nutritional economics, and nutrition and gerontology.

Career Prospects
Career prospects upon completing this degree can be found in local, national and international government, non-profit and private sectors with such titles as: clinical dietitian, registered dietitian, nutritionist, community health worker, health consultant, lecturer, health planner, health advocate and health researcher.

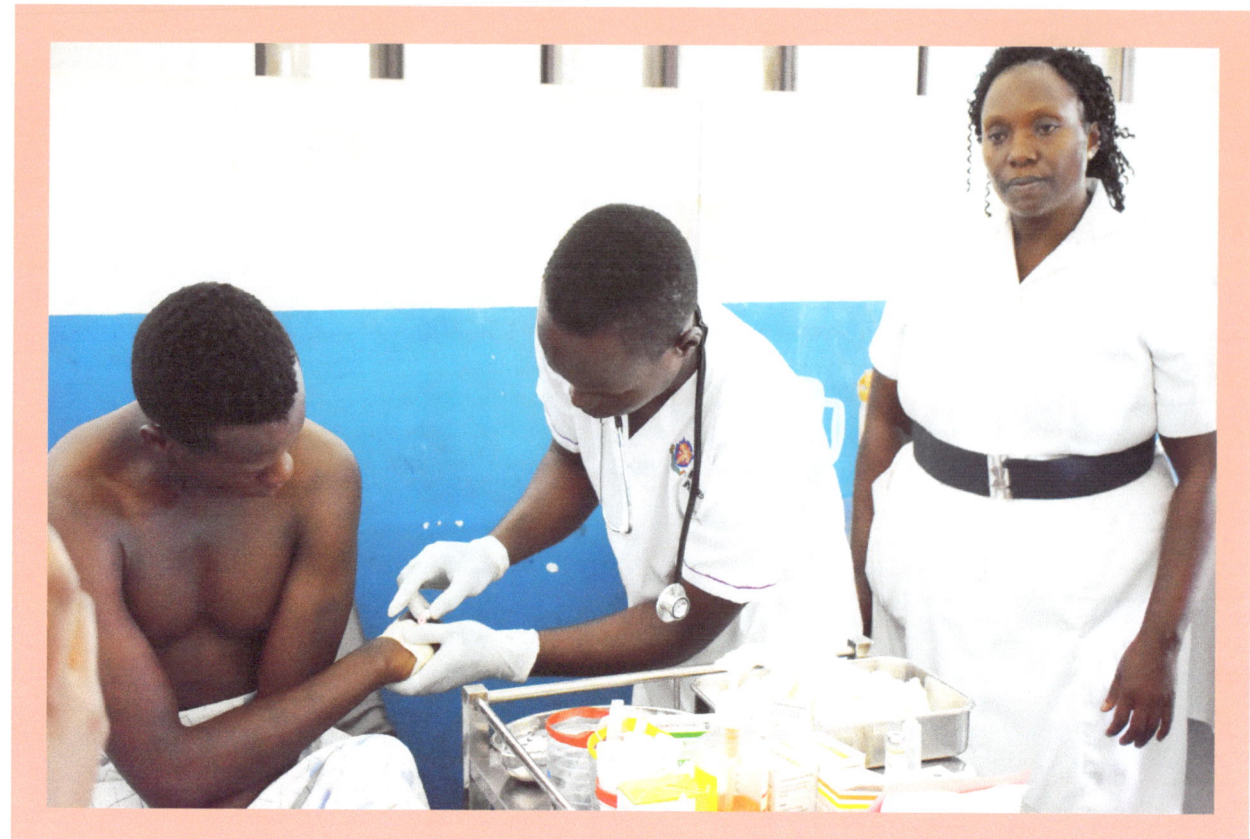

A UCU student administers medicine to a patient in the medical ward at Naguru Hospital while a senior nurse looks on

School of Medicine
Master of Public Health Leadership (MPHL)
Advent/ September Intake – Modular and Distance learning and research at Main/Mukono campus

Minimum Requirement
In order to be eligible for admission, candidates need the following:
- Holders of at least a bachelor's degree, or equivalent, from a recognized tertiary institution with a minimum of a second class degree (2:2);

Programme Length
Two years with up to 24 additional months to complete dissertation

Programme Highlights
The Master of Public Health Leadership Programme in the School of Medicine is best known under the title of Save The Mothers (STM), a Programme started by a Canadian Obstetrician, Dr. Jean Chamberlain in 2005 at Uganda Christian University (UCU) to improve the health and advocacy for pregnant and parenting women and survival of babies in Uganda. In this developing country, 97 percent of the health facilities do not offer adequate emergency obstetric care services. While the curriculum is centered around maternity issues, the knowledge and skill of the Programme is transferable to various employment sectors.

Courses
Content aimed at reducing the obstacles to safe childbirth in the following areas are included in the modules of the Programme, among others: research methods, financial management, networking, strategic communications, biostatistics, epidemiology and project planning.

Career Prospects
The Save The Mothers Programme has an initiative called Mother Baby Friendly Hospital that strives to place its master's graduates in various positions in government and private and nonprofit sectors. In addition to working in health care, graduates can get various positions to become advocates for change and to build new infrastructures.

SCHOOL OF RESEARCH AND POSTGRADUATE STUDIES

In 2020, the dean of the SRPGS is Associate Professor Kukunda Elizabeth Bacwayo (BA, PGD, MA, PhD). Heads of departments are Dr. Owor J. Jakisa, graduate studies; Associate Professor Peter Ubomba Jaswa, research; and Richard Sebaggala, Oil and Gas.

www.ucu.ac.ug/research/about-the-school-of-research

The Uganda Christian University School of Research and Postgraduate Studies (SRPGS) provides quality research and graduate academic services.

Our mission is to train and develop Christ-centered, globally competent scholars and professionals. As the oversight for research and postgraduate studies at UCU, this office promotes excellence in graduate education and training across the university in the areas of instruction, research and professional activity leading to the acquisition, creation and dissemination of new knowledge and the preparation of outstanding scholars and professionals.

The SRPGS aims to foster interdisciplinary research and teaching, and to help programmes prepare current graduate students as future leaders in teaching, research and development, applied science, policy making, and social service to Uganda and globally.

Instruments of Identity

As approved by the University Council in 2000, UCU students and staff are asked to adhere to these three areas (abbreviated from longer statements).
1. The Rule of Faith: Seeking to love God with all our heart, as He has revealed Himself
2. The Rule of Life: Seeking to love our neighbours as ourselves
3. The Rule of Prayer: Seeking to love God with all our soul and spirit

www.ingramcontent.com/pod-product-compliance
Lightning Source LLC
Chambersburg PA
CBHW041324290426

44108CB00005B/123